Cricut

2 Books in 1

The Most Complete Cricut Guide With Tips and Tricks To Design Space and Learn All The secret Of Your Machine

By

Mia Gomez

Rit
Rit
Rit
OVER
the Big
MOON

for any hardship or damages that may befall them after undertaking information described herein.

Additionally, the information in the following pages is intended only for informational purposes and should thus be thought of as universal. As befitting its nature, it is presented without assurance regarding its prolonged validity or interim quality. Trademarks that are mentioned are done without written consent and can in no way be considered an endorsement from the trademark holder.

Table Of Contents

CRICUT MAKER

CRICUT PROJECT

Cricut Maker

The Ultimate Guide To Cricut Maker With Tips and Tricks to Start Making Your Cricut Projects and Learn To Use Design Space

By

Mia Gomez

Cricut

Introduction

The Cricut machine was created and introduced into the market for a variety of reasons, including to make craftsmen's work easier and to assist others who wish to improve their art and design skills. Cricut was initially considered to have a small use, limited to scrapbooking. Later, because of its modern technologies and equipment, this myth was dispelled; it can do much more than only make scrapbooks; just the imagination can restrict it. People nowadays not only make their thoughts a practice, but they also profit from it.

The Cricut machine is a one-of-a-kind automated cutting machine for home craftsmen that can cut a variety of materials like silk, cloth, vinyl, wood, paper, and several others. This computer gadget also has the ability to cut and carve, engrave, deboss, and perforate. As a result, Cricut can be defined as an automated digital machine that can quickly generate your desired design on the necessary content. You must use your smartphone or other devices to sketch your desired design in the Cricut design room, then import it into the system and order it to execute its work. Cricut design space is software that gives users a forum with a lot of design opportunities so they can create their own designs using the resources in the software toolbar. The consumer must first download and update the design app, which is user-friendly and includes a range of design resources. After that, the consumer can move his or her designs from his or her mind to the designing app, then transfer the concept to the machine and click the run button to get a hardcopy of their imaginary design, thereby turning their vision into fact.

Chapter 1: What is Cricut?

Among the strongest instruments in an art toolkit are Cricut devices. They are used all the time to produce personalized t-shirts, greeting cards, posters, and a number of other crafts. In this chapter, you'll learn what there is to know about the Cricut cutting machines, how they operate, what they can perform and what materials you'll need to get started.

You may even be unsure which one of the 3 Cricut models is suitable for your requirements. Most beginners can start with the Cricut Explore Air 2 – but the Cricut Joy and Cricut Maker are both wonderful devices! Continue reading this book for a comparative study of the Cricut machines so you can make an informed decision on the right Cricut machine for you!

If you're a crafter who wants to do something, this is the book for you.

1.1 What Is A Cricut Machine?

A Cricut is an electrical machine that can cut various materials such as paper, card stock, vinyl, and iron-on transfers into various designs. Both leather and wood can be sliced with specific Cricut machines! Thin wood, leather, silk, and other materials may be sliced with certain Cricut machines. The Cricut can cut almost anything that will otherwise be cut with an X-acto knife or scissors. However, a Cricut can cut with much greater accuracy and speed than can be achieved by hand!

A cutting machine of Cricut can be compared to a home printer. Instead of printing the design on a paper sheet, a Cricut machine cuts the design from a sheet of paper using a thin, movable blade (or other material.)

1.2 Blades For Cricut

As previously said, the Cricut machine will cut over 300 different materials. However, since each substance has its own set of features, the blades used to cut it are often special. Cricut Maker is the most sophisticated machine on the Cricut line. It has the most blades that can be used for its hardware. The great part regarding the Cricut Maker is that as Cricut releases new blades in the future, they will all be compliant with the Cricut Maker. Investing in the Cricut Manufacturer, then, could prove to be a wise choice.

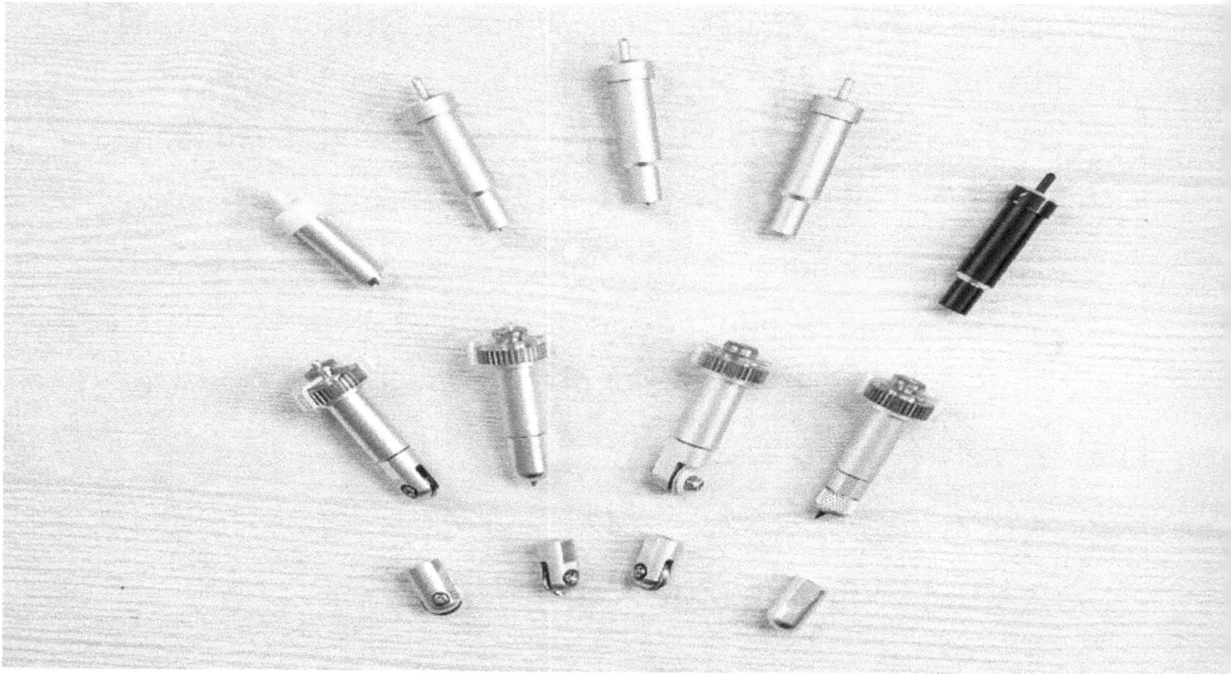

1.3 The Most Successful Cutting Machines

Die-cutter machines and craft plotters are terms used to describe machines like the Cricut. Silhouette Cameo and Brother ScanNCut are two other cutting machine brands.

The Cricut Maker, The Cricut Explore Air 2, and the Cricut Joy are the three models of Cricut machines currently available.

The Cricut Explore Air 2 is the most common and mid-level computer. The Maker is a huge upgrade from the Explore Air 2 in terms of material cutting capabilities. The Joy is the most recent gadget, and it's a smaller, compact model that's simple to set up and operate.

1.4 How Do They Work?

Your dream will become a fact with only a little effort, thanks to all of these features. The blades and tools can be overwhelming to a first-time Cricut Maker user. For others, the prospect of learning and operating modern technologies may be terrifying. But don't be concerned. We've taken care of it.

Any Cricut machine comes with a comprehensive online manual and other sources of various Cricut tools, making them relatively simple to learn how to use. Both the Cricut machines and Design Space are designed to be simple to use, and you don't need a lot of graphic design knowledge to use them (It does, however, assist you in creating your own creations from scratch). In Cricut's Design Room, there's a library of designs and images that you can easily import as a new project. Some are unrestricted, while others can be bought for a small fee.

To begin, use Cricut's design app or software to build a design. Then, using Bluetooth or USB, you submit the specification to the Cricut cutting unit. The template is fed into the Cricut system, which then cuts it out with a thin, precise cutter.

You may use a wireless connection to link a Cricut to your device, make or save designs on your computer, and then send them to your Cricut to cut. Design Space (Windows, MAC, and smart mobile phone) is Cricut's app that helps you to build and import templates to cut with your machine. A tiny blade (rotary cutter, scoring tool or pen) is housed within the Cricut. After you've created a design in Design Space, you can place your preferred material on a 12 inch wide cutting mat, wirelessly transfer your design to your Cricut, and then insert your material into your unit. Your project will start cutting as soon as you click a button.

1.5 Here's how to use a Cricut

1. Begin by placing the cutting material on the sticky cutting pad. (While the Cricut performs the cuts, the cutting pad keeps the material in place.) Place the mat in the unit and turn it on.

2. Next, open Cricut Design Space and choose a design. Send the pattern to your Cricut cutting machine after selecting your content settings.

3. To begin cutting, hit the button on the Cricut machine.

4. Detach the mat from the machine and the product from the mat once the machine has finished cutting.

Learning how to use a Cricut by watching videos is a fantastic way to get started. On Cricut's website, you can also find a lot of useful video tutorials.

1.6 Are Cricut machines worth it?

A Cricut machine is a wise purchase if you enjoy crafting, particularly with paper and vinyl. It will make your cut designs look smooth and professional, and once you've mastered it, it will make your crafts go even faster. You can also make money for your Cricut by selling personalized t-shirts, mugs, decals, and other items online or at art fairs.

1.7 From where can you buy these?

Cricuts can be purchased directly from Cricut's website, or you can order the devices and accessories from Amazon. To shop for Cricut, go on Amazon. Cricut machines and accessories are available at craft stores, including Michaels and JOANN.

Chapter 2: What can I make with Cricut?

You will do a lot of interesting things with your Cricut. In certain instances, this is sufficient justification for purchasing a machine. "The minute you need a tool, it's already paying for itself" if you remember this, you will never hesitate to purchase tools.

And if you are purchasing the computer for personal use and have no intention of selling your work, it is a very cost-effective purchase. Anything from cutting shapes and patterns for school assignments to designing personalized presents, cutting vinyl for home decor, and simply wearing leather jewelry! There are many advantages that can save you money in the long run.

It's almost as if you are paying rent to sit at your desk. If you want to make sure, it will really pay for itself. Here are five ways to benefit from your Cricut machine:

2.1 Sell Cut Vinyl

It will only take a few months for you to recoup the cost of your first unit. If you don't have a large site so start an Etsy store for your products. You don't have to make an effort to publicize it. They will just discover it! Consider how much more money you will make if you are promoted a bit more!

Pinterest is a great place to post your Etsy listings because it attracts a lot of traffic. There are guidelines for using Cricut Design Space stock photographs, but you cannot sell them. Basically, market the products you make. Make something that is completely special to you. The customer could choose the words that would be printed on the product.

Another cool vinyl item to market is bumper stickers. People enjoy adorning their vehicles with fandom, geekery, and other nonsense. Make one sticker of each style you're considering, photograph it, and put it on the market. You should make another if there is more demand!

The best part of selling vinyl is how simple it is to ship; most items can be sent in a single package. It's that easy!

2.2 Sell Finished Pieces

The concept is the same as in #1. Here's a perfect way to do it: make projects for your computer. Create two of something interesting you make, such as an art piece, a onesie, wall art, or t-shirt, or jewelry. Make double of everything. One to hold or give as a gift, and the other to sell. This way, programs will continue to pay for themselves.

Put them up for sale on Etsy or other handmade marketplaces. Projects like these watercolor signs are really common right now! (And they don't necessitate anything in the way of inventiveness).

OR

Custom cake toppers are able to be sold. They're totally on board. They're simple to make and cut with the Cricut, and they're small enough to ship for a reasonable price!

2.3 Use Social Media To Sell Custom Jobs!

These days, social media is a massive source of money. If you're selling something, there are plenty of hashtags to use: #forsale #selling #product...just by using these, users will ask about purchasing. There are several Facebook groups and pages dedicated to selling homemade items...just look for them and join. Add the things to the list.

You can also post items on your personal website, such as "I will cut personalized vinyl for someone who is keen, just so you know." This is another way to get a little extra money.

Simply add a photo of a project you've completed, whether it's a vinyl cut or something else, and let people know you'd love to sell it if someone is interested. You'll be pleasantly shocked! Especially during the holiday season. (Get the computer now and start making gifts for the holidays!)

2.4 Make Money By Selling Iron-On Vinyl.

Iron-on is a great deal! It's the same concept as selling vinyl. It's simple to package, and all you have to do is provide instructions about how to use it on the requested stuff. Every month, all of these factors come together to make a significant difference.

You can also market finished iron-on vinyl parts. Get some cheap bulk bags and iron on some nice patterns. Create collections for birthday party favors, summer camps, and other occasions. Everyone adores personalized work, such as monograms and initials.

T-shirts for family gatherings and theme park visits! To make shirts for friends, colleagues, families, and others, simply use Iron-on Vinyl/Heat Transfer Vinyl. Charge for the vinyl as well as the time spent on it. They looked amazing and received a lot of compliments on their outing! You can't sell licensed themed products, so stay away from Harry Potter, Star Wars, Disney, the BBC, and everything else advertised.

2.5 Go To different places To Sell Your Products!

Set up a store! This one isn't always "at home." When you put up a boutique or a booth, you are restricted by the number of customers who will come, and you would hope that they will all want to purchase your pieces. It's possible! The other problem is the setup, booth displays, large quantities of inventory, packaging, and transportation.

2.6 Still, What If I'm Not A Creative Person?

This is an expression mostly heard from people. Here is an advice to them "You are just as creative as your tools." Of course, you won't be crafty if all you have at home are crayons and child coloring books. You'll be shocked by how crafty you get if you have the tools to do fun crafts. Get the unit and the starter kit, and start crafting right away!

Here's the deal: You don't need to be a crafty person to enjoy and use this gadget. It practically takes care of anything for you. Consider the benefits and drawbacks and purchase a Cricut.

Chapter 3: Types of Cricut machines

Cricut machines are currently available in three different models: Cricut Explore Air 2, Cricut Maker, and Cricut Joy (this is the latest model).

You've landed in the right place if you're trying to figure out which Cricut machine is best for you. To support your decision, here's a comparison of Cricut Maker, Cricut Joy, and Cricut Explore Air 2.

What computer you purchase can be determined by the kinds of projects you choose to complete. Cricut's Design Space app is included with all these machines for free.

3.1 Cricut Explore Air 2

This is the machine I'd use for the majority of projects. It's Cricut's most famous gadget, and it'll cut vinyl, cloth, cardstock, and chipboard, among other products, for a broad range of DIY projects. This computer can cut almost 100 materials and has four instruments for cutting, printing, and scoring.

The best-selling Cricut Explore Air 2 cutting machines make DIY simple, interesting, and awesome, with the versatility to cut out a broad selection of craft materials and the accuracy to produce precisely what you need.

For fans of well-known materials

For a reason, it is the best-selling unit! It will cut vinyl, cardstock, iron-on, and backed cotton, among other products.

DIYers who want to work on a mega project

The "most important" distinction between full-size machines and Cricut Joy is size. When you want to cut a material between 4.25 to 12 inches, use the Cricut Explore Air 2 or Cricut Maker.

For quick-thinking creators

You'll enjoy Quick Mode whether you're in a pinch or really want to make use of your time. It allows you to cut and write up to 2 times quicker. When dealing with common materials such as vinyl, cardstock and iron-on, it doubles the tempo. Quick Mode is available on both the Cricut Explore Air 2 and Cricut Maker.

For colorful crafters

The Cricut Explore Air 2 has a broad range of shades, which is one of the favorite things about it, which includes Wild Rose and Flamingo Pearl, as well as Emerald, Peach Kiss, Peacock, and also the Cherry Blossom.

Cricut Explore Air 2 can be the computer for you if you want to convey your imagination by coloring your craft area.

3.2 Cricut Maker

This gadget contains all of the features of the Cricut Explore Air 2, including the ability to cut thicker or more fragile materials, including leather, thin woods, and fabrics and 10X the cutting capacity. With this unit, you can cut nearly 300 materials and use over Dozen tools for cutting, recording, scoring, and other pro-level effects. If you'd like to try more complex tasks and play with a broader variety of materials, this computer is a good choice.

For next-level makers

Cricut Maker gives you more options in terms of equipment, products, and possibilities. Cricut Maker has an expandable toolset that includes denser, thicker materials, the Knife Blade, for unbacked and backed fabric, Rotary Blade, and for debossing, engraving, scoring, and incorporating cosmetic effects, the Quick Swap bunch of tools.

For multi-dimensional DIYers

Cricut Maker is ideal for making structural components for 3D designs, such as templates, furniture, and more, since it can cut heavier, denser materials.

For passionate sewers

If you want to sew or imagine you could sometime, Cricut Maker will assist you with the most complex and time-consuming aspects of the process: cutting and labeling pattern bits. You may also add sewing designs to the site belonging to only you.

For smart quilters

Quilters enjoy Cricut Maker because it allows them to cut out quilt and appliqué bits precisely, so they are able to concentrate on the enjoyable material.

For the stylish and sleek

The streamlined design of the Cricut Maker with a shimmery, shiny finish and is available in five sophisticated colors (Champagne, Rose, Blue, Lilac and Mint).

3.3 Cricut Joy

Cricut Joy, the latest Cricut machine, is a more versatile machine than the other two, making it ideal for simple, daily DIY projects. It will only cut materials up to 5.5 inches high, so you can buy really long materials (up to 20 feet). It can cut and write with two tools and can cut and write over 50 different materials. If you want to save money and make simple projects such as vinyl posters, cards, and tiny iron-on designs, this gadget is suggested.

Cricut Joy, your new DIY best friend

Cricut Joy cuts and writes for you much like full-size Cricut computers. It will cut without a cutting pad, including materials you possibly use at home (construction paper, copy paper, etc.), traditional crafting materials (iron-on, vinyl, Infusible Ink, etc.), and modern Smart Materials. It's the ideal complement to any Cricut machine and a pleasant way to get started with DIY.

For those that like to conserve space and are always on the run

Cricut Joy would blend right in whether you live in a condo, a tiny home, or just enjoy the simplicity of limited spaces. Quite literally. It fits neatly in a cubby, looks nice on a fridge, is simple to store, and sets up quickly.

For extra-long project

Cricut Joy is compact enough to fit in the middle of one hand, but it can cut continuous forms up to 4 inches wide and 4 ft long or create repeated cuts up to 20 feet long, thanks to Smart Materials.

For last-minute makers

It is said that Cricut Joy sets up quickly, which is especially useful when you're pressed for time. It also fits with the latest pre-scored Insert Cards, allowing you to quickly create a personalized card before a wedding, a birthday party, or a baby shower.

In Design Room, you'll also find a slew of new projects designed especially for Cricut Joy that take less than 15 minutes to complete. This little beauty is for you if you're short of time.

For both experienced and inexperienced organizers

Smart Label Paper and Smart Label Vinyl are two of most favorite Smart Materials for Cricut Joy. They make organization easy, enjoyable, and exciting. Cricut Joy writes in any font directly on Smart Label, cuts it into any form you specify, and all you have to do now is peel and stick.

You can already see it: an orderly line of herbs, well-organized pantry cabinets, and clean plastic bins that don't need to be opened to see what's inside.

To compare all Cricut machines, click the picture below.

	Cricut Joy™ Simple & compact	Cricut Explore Air® 2 Our most popular machine	Cricut Maker® The ultimate smart cutting machine
Perfect for	Quick, everyday, fun projects	A wide range of DIY hobbies	Pro-level DIY performance & versatility
Max material width	5.5 in	12 in	12 in
Max material length	20 ft	2 ft	2 ft
Material compatibility	50+ materials	100+ materials	300+ materials
Tools / Capabilities	2 (for cutting & writing)	5+ (for cutting, writing, scoring)	12+ (for cutting, writing, scoring, debossing, engraving & more)
Commercial-grade performance	—	—	✓
Works with Smart Materials for long, continuous cuts without a cutting mat	✓	—	—
Works with Card Mat for quick custom cards	✓	—	—
Works with home printer to print, then cut out printed image perfectly	—	✓	✓
Free design app for iOS, Android™ Windows®, and Mac®	✓	✓	✓
Connectivity	Bluetooth®	Bluetooth®, USB	Bluetooth®, USB

Chapter 4: Cricut Installation

The Cricut Maker is available in a variety of bundles, including the Everything Bundle option and the Essential bundle option. The Essential Bundle options come with all you need to get started on a new project. Cricut vinyl, Cricut textured board, and Cricut cardstock is examples of these. Similarly, the Everything Bundle option tools to get you started on new ideas right away. We'll go over all of the standard Cricut Maker features as well as what comes standard with a simple Cricut Maker.

4.1 Unboxing of the Cricut Maker

You have arrived at the most thrilling aspect of your journey. The Unboxing of the Cricut Maker. The Cricut Maker is currently available in 5 different colors:

1. Lilac
2. Rose
3. Blue
4. Champagne
5. Mint

You'll notice the following items when you open your Cricut Maker:

- Cricut Maker machine
- One black fine tip pen
- Instruction Booklet
- 50 free projects in Design Space for practice
- Power adapter
- Materials for a practice project
- USB cable
- Pink Colored Fabric Grip Mat (Standard Size)
- Light Grip Machine Mat (Standard Size)
- Rotary blade with housing
- Trial membership for Design Access (Free)
- Fine point blade with housing

The fine point blade and housing are often already installed in the Cricut Maker. But don't be concerned if you can't seem to find it straight away. To begin, look inside the Cricut Maker. The blade is most likely already in position.

Design Space is available for Windows and Mac computers, as well as iOS and Android devices. The following are the minimum standards that are recommended.

- Mac
- Windows
- Apple iOS

- Google Android

Important: To download and sign in to this program, you must have access to the internet.

To get Design Space for Desktop for your Windows device, follow these steps:

1. Open a tab and browse to design.cricut.com.

2. Click on the Download button. The screen can shift during the download. Per browser would be a little different in this regard. In this case, Google Chrome is used.

3. Double-click the file in the tab or in your Downloads folder when it's finished downloading.

4. Whether a window appears asking if you want to trust the application, click the option to trust it.

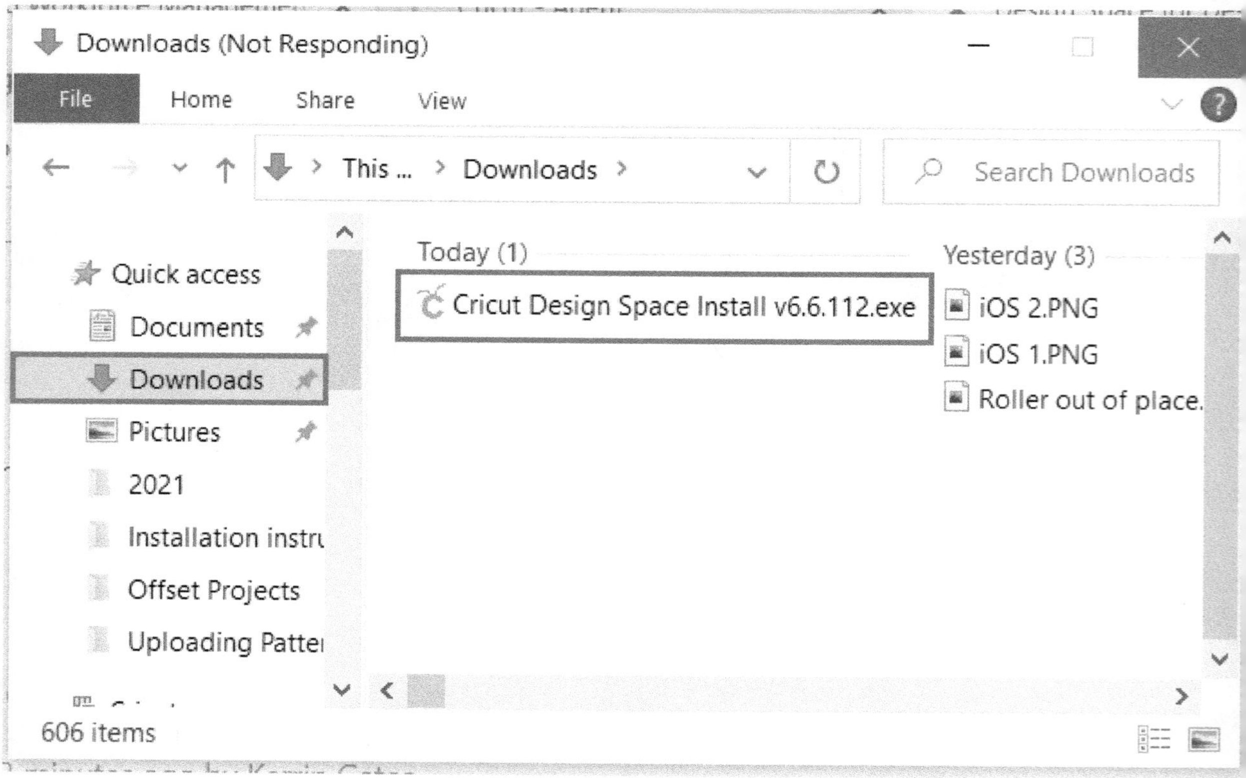

5. The installation progress is shown in a setup window.

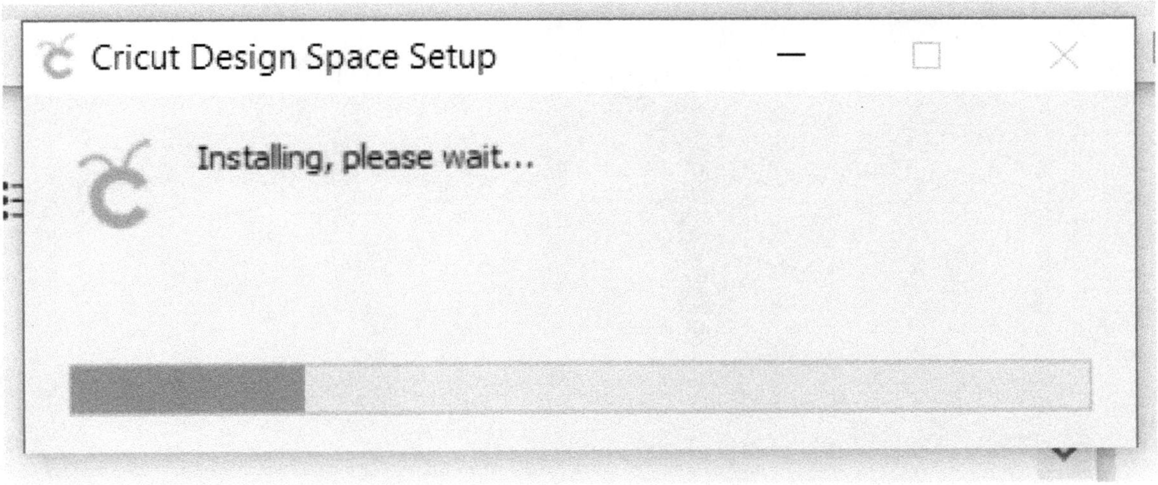

6. Enter your Cricut ID and password to log in.

7. A Design Space for Desktop icon appears on the Desktop automatically. To pin the shortcut to the Taskbar, right-click upon this icon and select Pin to Taskbar, or move the icon to the Taskbar.

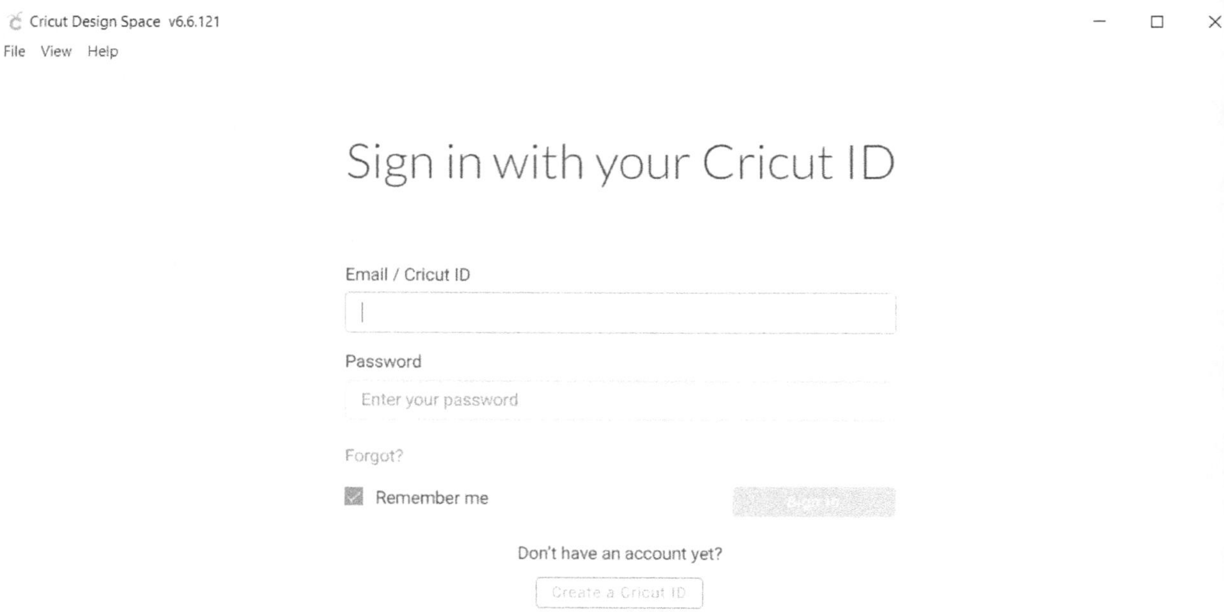

8. Take pleasure in utilizing Design Space for Desktop!

4.2 Things to know

- The software remembers the sign-in details.
- The software does not auto-save, so you would have to sign in each time you open it because you opted

out of the previous session. When you plan, save the tasks regularly and until exiting the program.

4.3 Procedure for setting up Cricut Maker or Cricut Explore

When you finish the setup, the machine is automatically registered to your account. Follow these measures to set up your Cricut Explore, Explore Air, Explore One, Cricut Maker or Explore Air 2 machine:

- Windows and Macintosh
- Apple iOS/Android

1. Switch on the computer by plugging it in.

2. Use the USB cord to connect the unit to your phone or pair it with Bluetooth.

3. Open the window and go to design.cricut.com/setup.

4. Get Design Space for Desktop and install it.

5. Sign in or generate a Cricut ID, then set up the new machine by following the on-screen directions.

6. When you're asked to take a test cut, you'll realize the configuration is final.

During system initialization, the machine is automatically registered. Reconnect your system, go to design.cricut.com/config or pick New Machine Setup from the Design Space account menu, and obey the on-screen instructions if you did not finish setup when you first linked your machine to your device.

4.4 Attaching Cricut Maker or Cricut Explore to a Bluetooth device

With the Cricut Explore and Cricut Maker computers, you can cut off wirelessly. To connect them with your mobile or machine, follow the measures below:

To sever wirelessly, the Cricut Explore one and/or Cricut Explore need a Bluetooth Adapter that should be wireless.

- • iOS
- • Android
- • Windows
- • Mac

1. Make sure your Cricut Maker or Cricut Explore system is turned on and next to your screen (about 10 to 15 feet). Make sure your Bluetooth Adapter (Wireless) is inserted whether you have a Cricut Explore One or simple Cricut Explore.

2. Bluetooth is supported by the majority of devices. However, click the right button on the Start icon and tap Device Manager to see if your machine is Bluetooth-enabled.

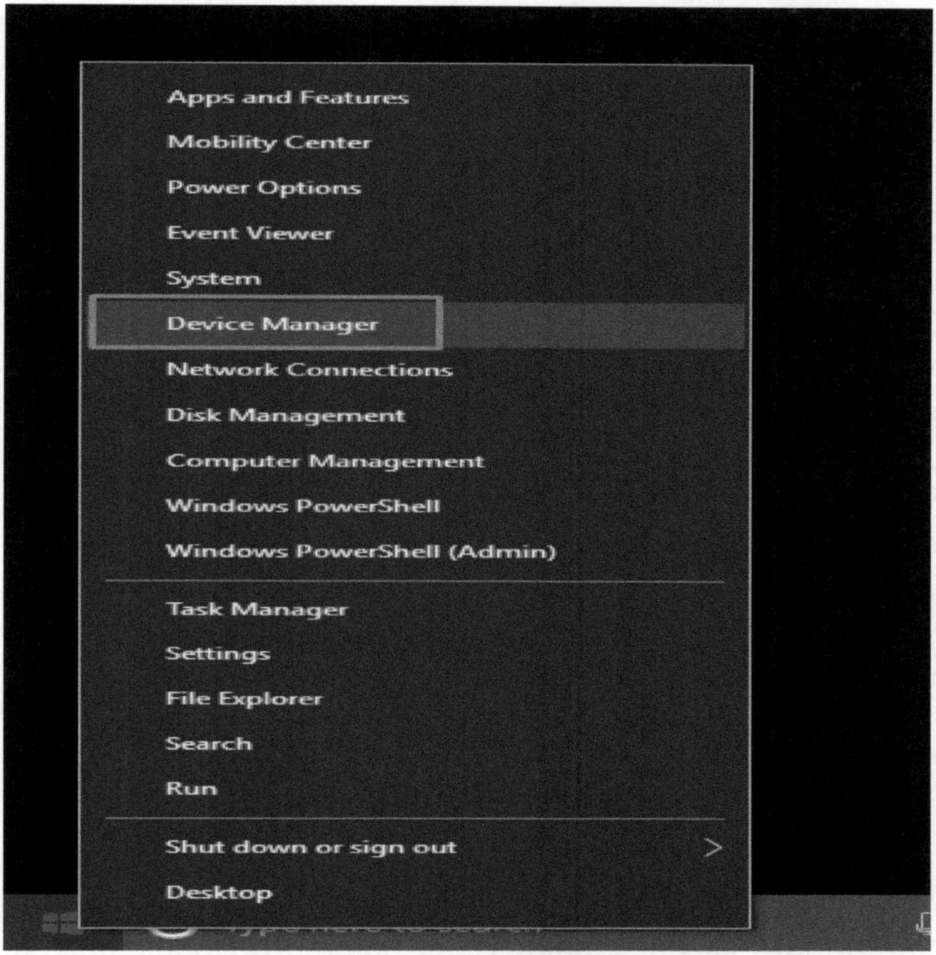

3. Your device is Bluetooth activated if Bluetooth is identified. If not, you'll need to buy a Bluetooth Dongle, which is a device having a USB port that allows your machine to communicate with other devices containing Bluetooth.

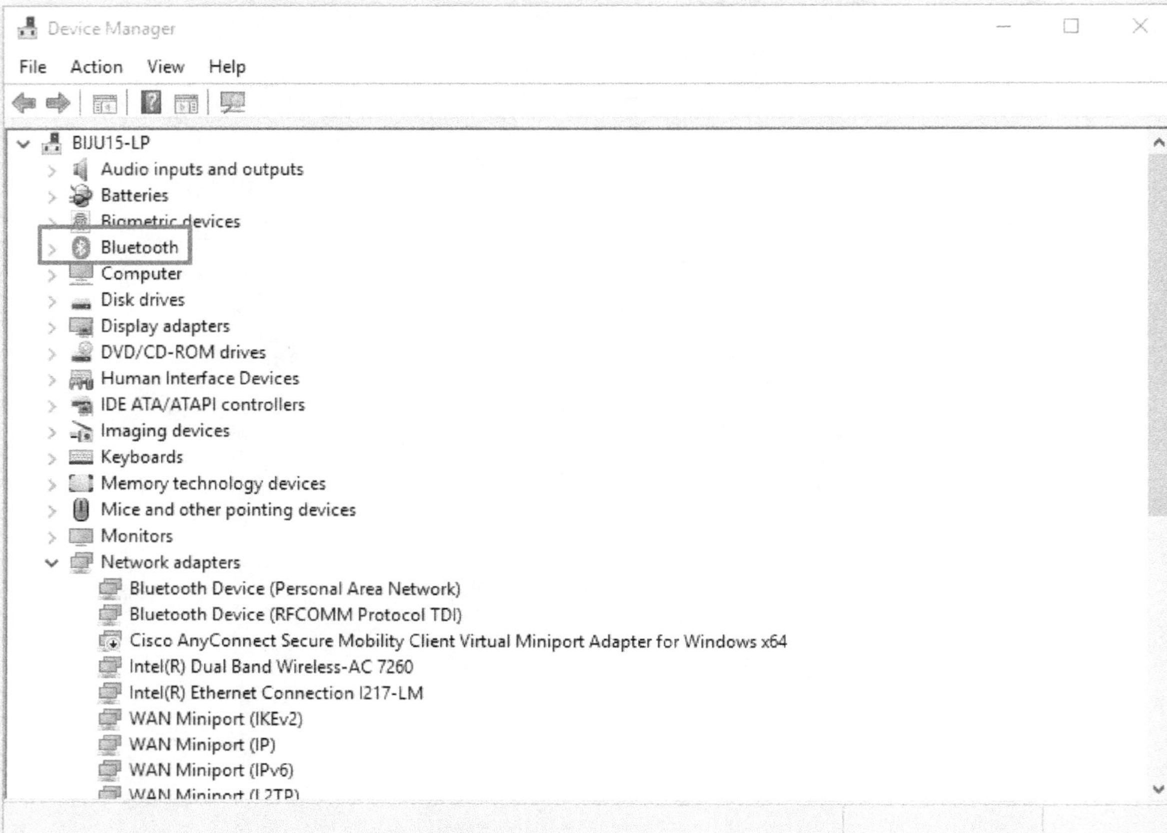

Cambridge Silicone Radio (CSR) Bluetooth Dongles are not compatible with Cricut devices, according to the research. It is recommended to get a Bluetooth dongle that helps audio devices if you need one for your phone. While it is not ensured that all the dongles would work with Cricut devices, those that help audio devices are most of the time effective.

4. Shut down Device Manager.

5. Pick Settings from the Start menu at the bottom of your screen.

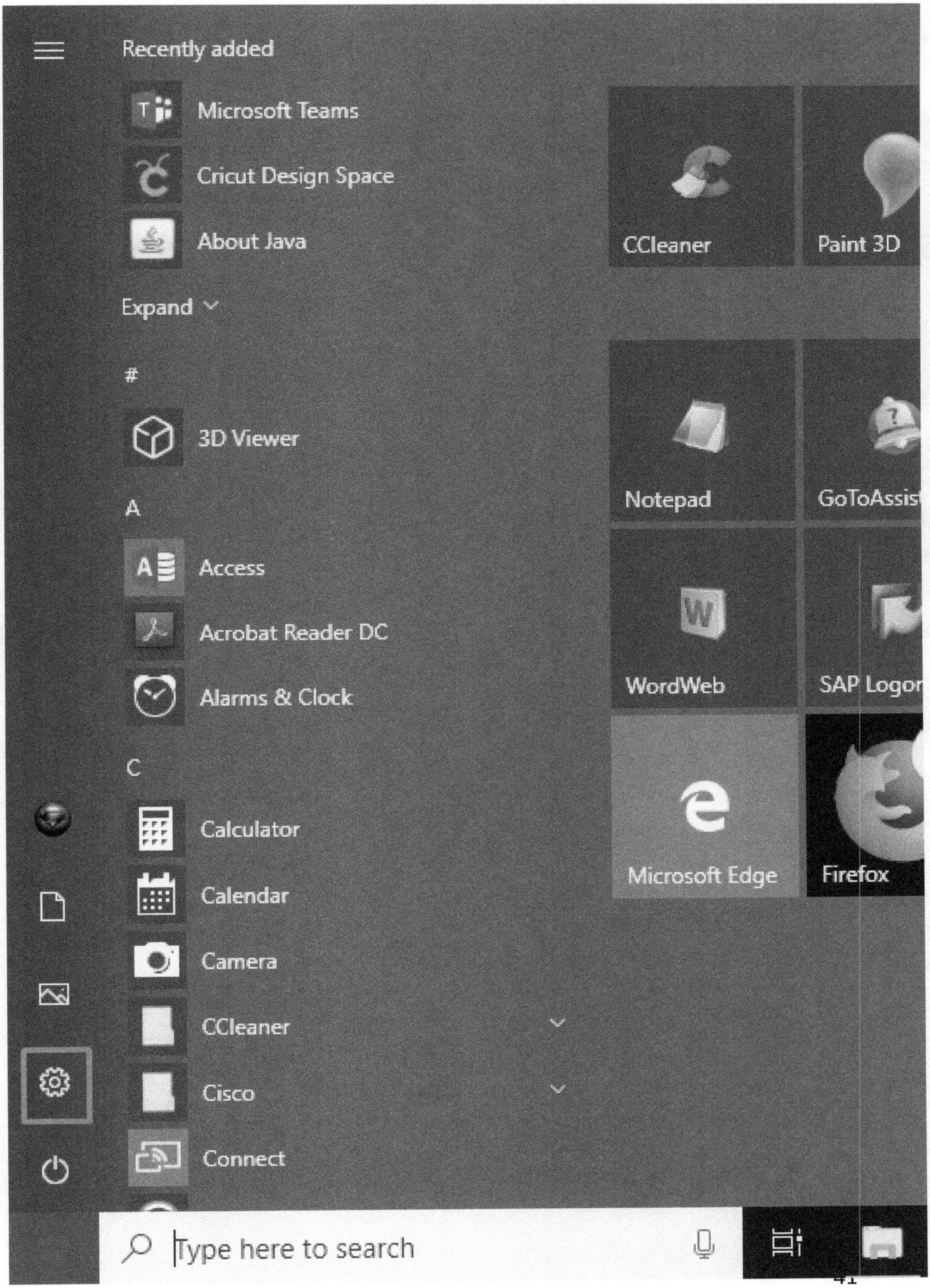
Recently added
Microsoft Teams
Cricut Design Space
About Java
Expand
#
3D Viewer
A
Access
Acrobat Reader DC
Alarms & Clock
C
Calculator
Calendar
Camera
CCleaner
Cisco
Connect
CCleaner
Paint 3D
Notepad
GoToAssist
WordWeb
SAP Logon
Microsoft Edge
Firefox
Type here to search

6. Choose Devices from the drop-down menu.

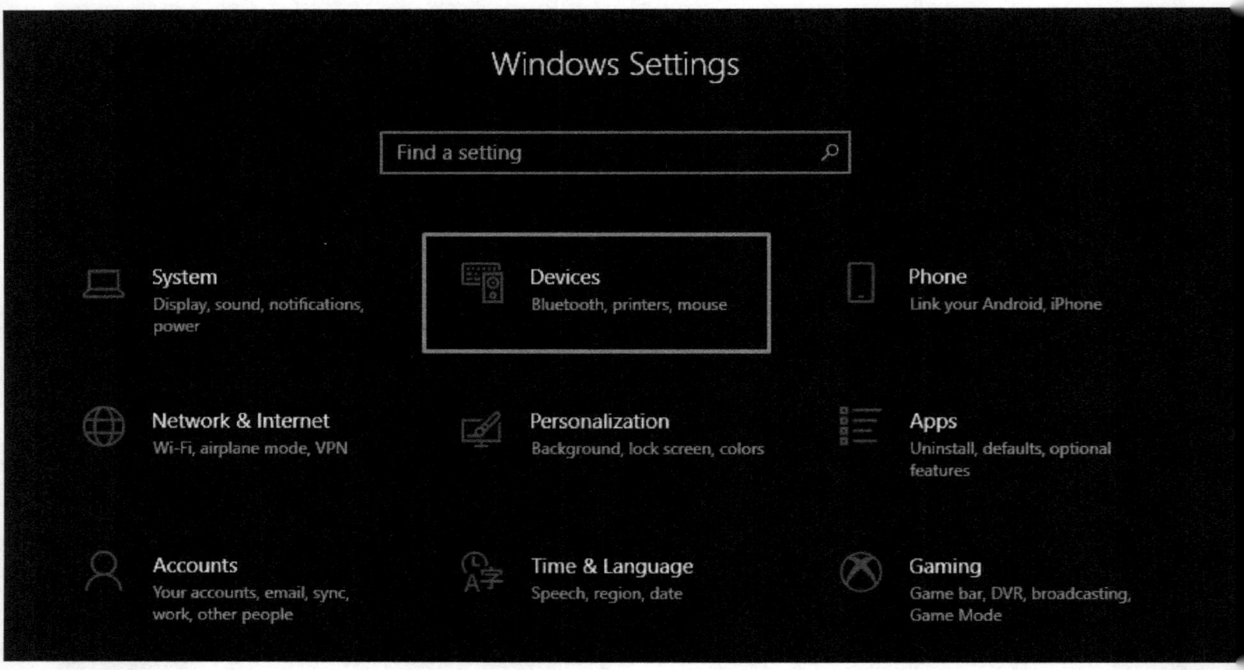

7. Make sure Bluetooth is turned on, and then choose "Add Bluetooth or another device."

8. Press the Bluetooth button and just wait for a few seconds for the device to recognize the Cricut machine. Choose your computer from the drop-down menu.

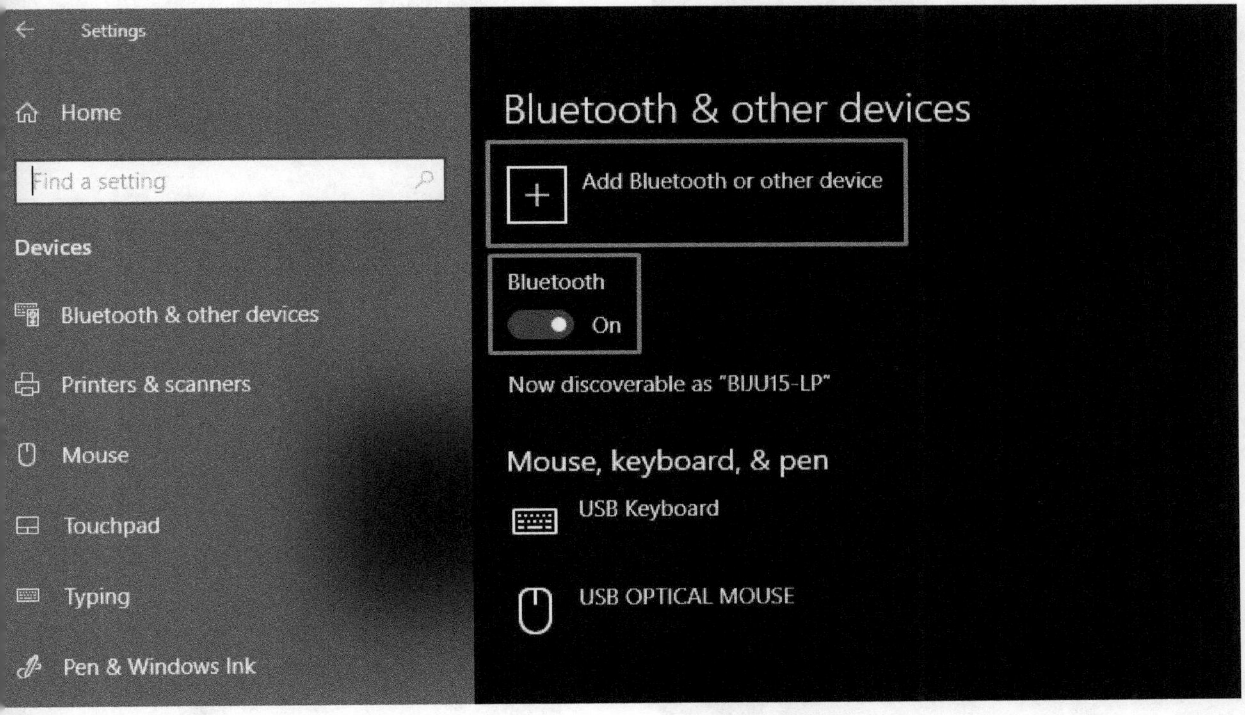

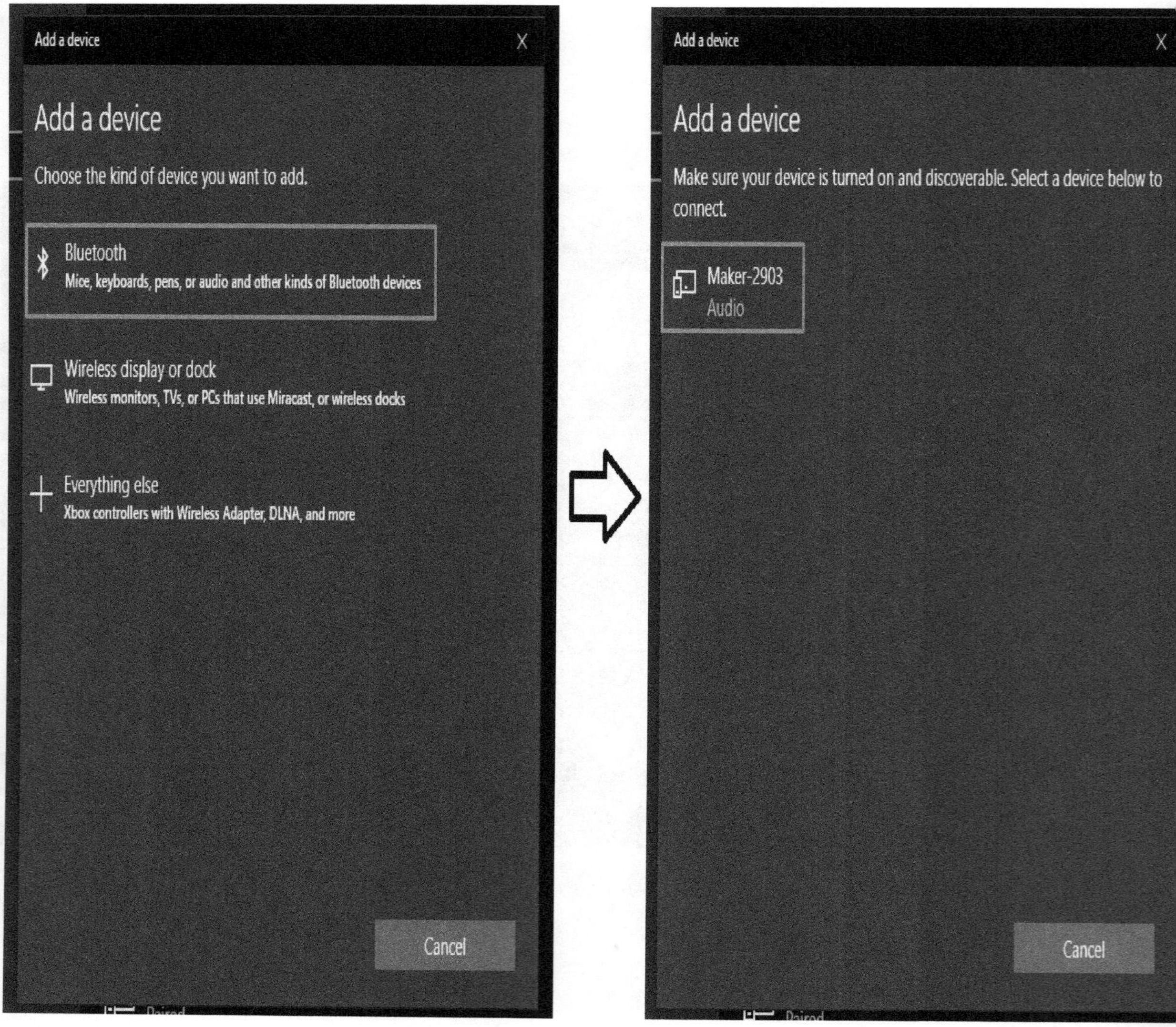
Add a device
Add a device
Choose the kind of device you want to add.
Bluetooth
Mice, keyboards, pens, or audio and other kinds of Bluetooth devices
Wireless display or dock
Wireless monitors, TVs, or PCs that use Miracast, or wireless docks
Everything else
Xbox controllers with Wireless Adapter, DLNA, and more
Cancel
Add a device
Add a device
Make sure your device is turned on and discoverable. Select a device below to connect.
Maker-2903
Audio
Cancel

9. If you're asked for a PIN, enter 0000. After that, choose Link.

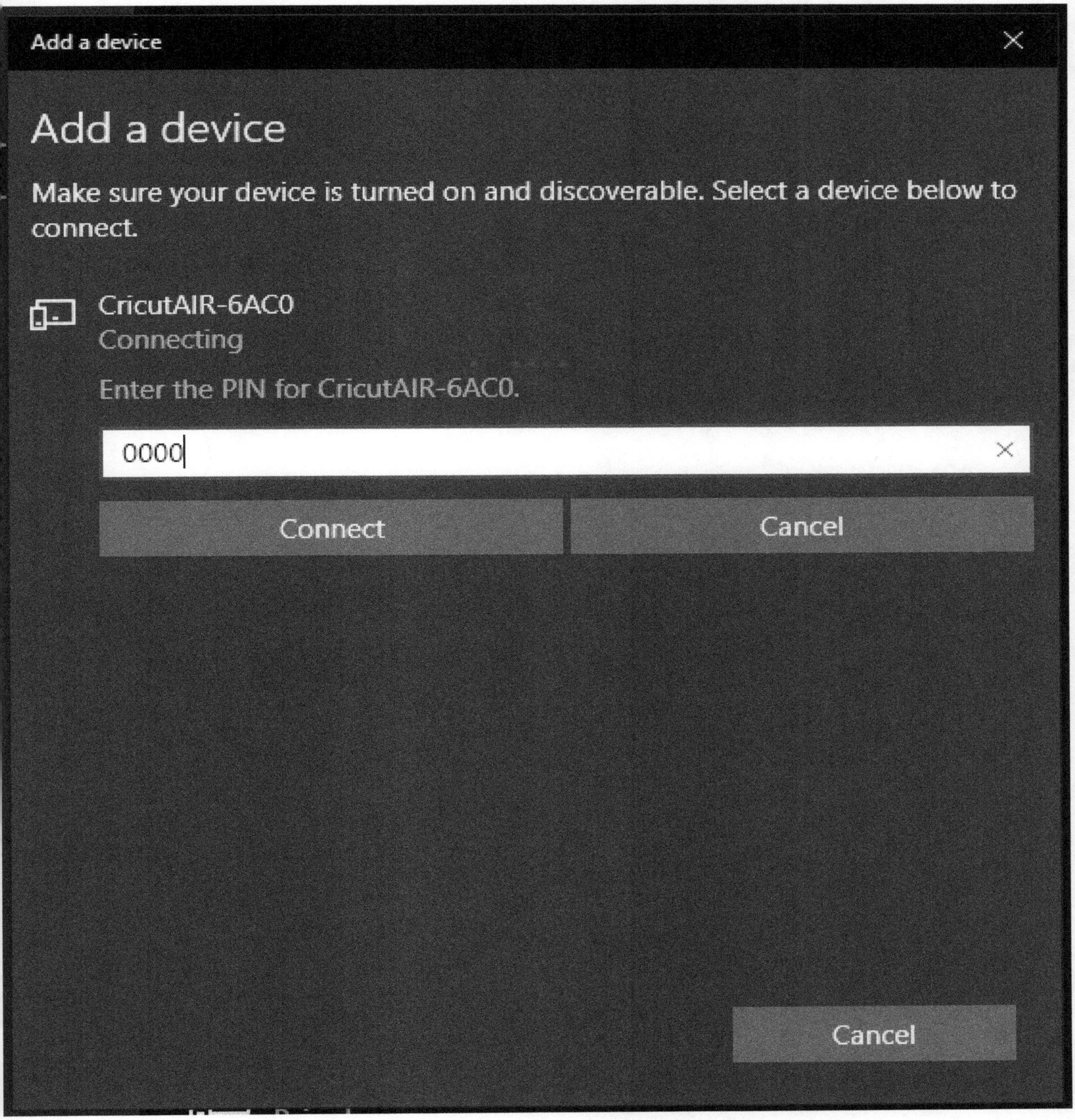

10. Your Cricut Explore or Cricut Maker is now connected to your screen running Windows!

It's common for Cricut Explore or Cricut Maker machines to appear in the list as Audio. If you have several Cricut machines, use the system code to find the one you want to combine. This can be seen on the serial number sticker on the back of the container.

These instructions and screen-shots are only from Windows 10. If you require assistance with a particular Windows operating system, please feel free to contact Member-Care.

4.5 Uninstalling Cricut Design Space

Please take the measures below to delete Design Space from your machine or mobile for troubleshooting purposes or permanently:

- Windows
- iOS
- Mac
- Android

1. Make sure the Design Space for the Desktop is turned off. The program would not uninstall correctly if it is not closed.

2. Click the Start button in the bottom left-hand corner of the computer and type Programs into the search box. Select the Add or Remove Programs function. The Apps & Features window will appear.

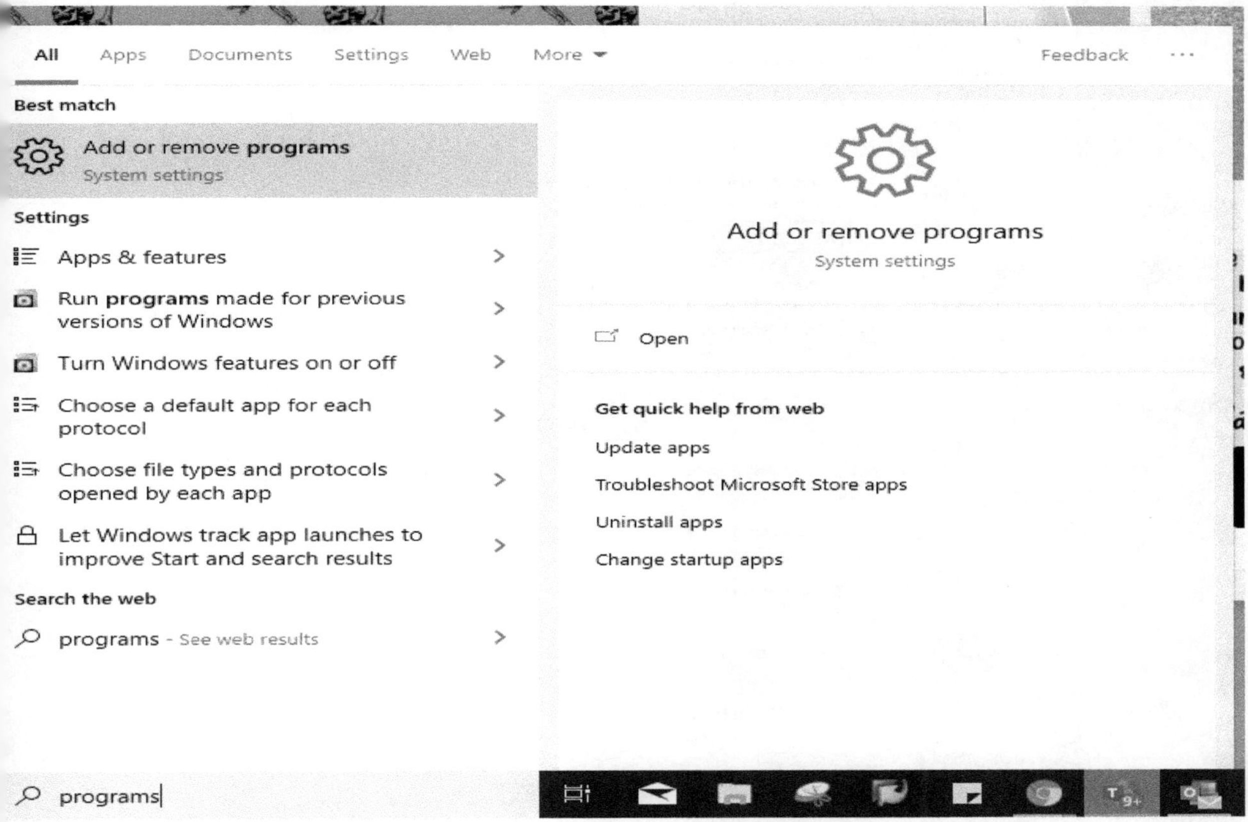

3. Type "Cricut" into the search area. Pick Cricut Design Space from the drop-down menu, then click Uninstall.

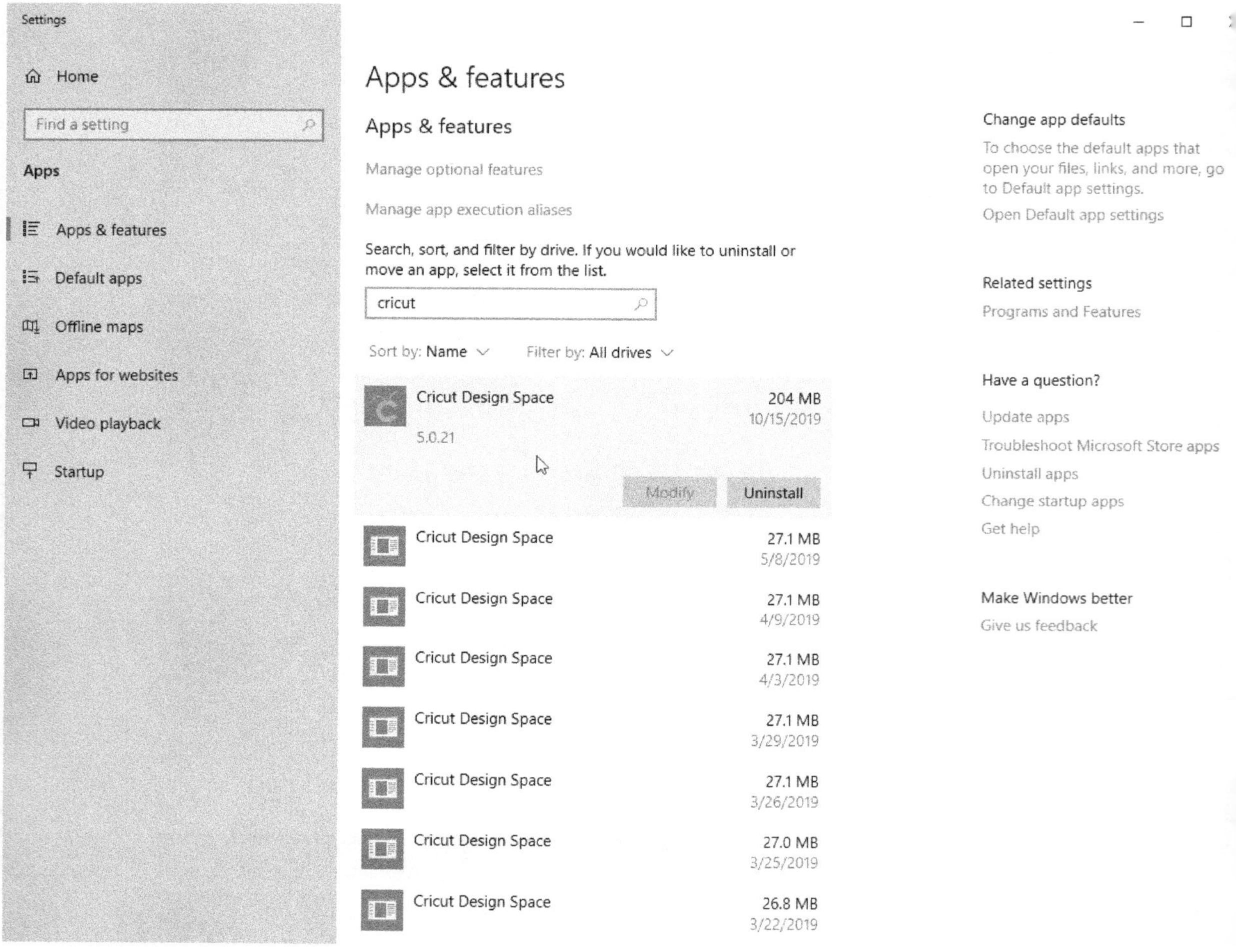

4. Verify that you choose to uninstall Cricut Design Room.

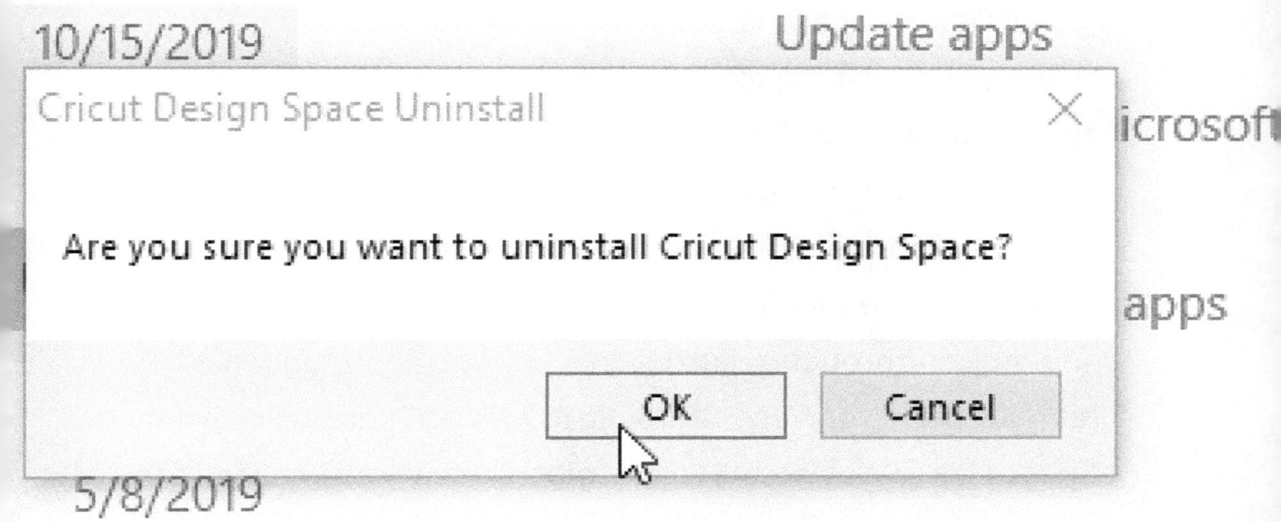

5. The uninstallation will be completed by the system. Restart the machine if asked.

Notice that depending on the Windows edition, there might be minor differences. For more details, go to windows.microsoft.com.

Tip: Once you've uninstalled programs from your machine, it's a good idea to restart the computer before reinstalling them.

Chapter 5: Design Space Application

Cricut Design Space is a companion program for the Cricut Maker and Cricut Explore machines that allows you to design and cut wirelessly. Create a startup or visit the Cricut Image Library for thousands of files, predesigned Make It Now projects, and fonts. You can view your projects and photos anytime you're motivated since the software is cloud-based and synced through your devices. To imagine the idea on a real-life backdrop, use the built-in video. Then, using your Cricut Maker or Cricut Explore machine's wireless Link, cut your designs!

5.1 Features

• Build DIY projects with the Cricut Maker and Cricut Explore cutting machines.

• Choose from the Cricut Picture Library's over 50,000 photographs, fonts, and projects—or use your own photos and fonts for free.

• Upload and edit your own photos

• Use fonts and icons downloaded to your computer to design and cut without the need for an Internet link.

• Make home and party decoration, cards and invites, scrapbooking, fashion, jewelry, kids' crafts, and more with simple and simple predesigned Make It Now projects

• Use your device's built-in camera to pose and imagine your designs on a real-life backdrop

• Cut a broad range of fabrics, like paper, acrylic, cardstock, iron-on, fabric, poster board—even tougher materials including leather

• Sign in with your Cricut ID to view your photographs and projects, as well as to make transactions on Cricut.com and in Design Space more convenient.

• Wireless capability via Bluetooth® (wireless Bluetooth adapter may be needed, sold separately).

If your life revolves around crafting and making using the best materials available. Whenever anything fresh is published, you fully try it to fail miserably. The latest Cricut Design Space App is for you. The latest Cricut Design Space App isn't half bad. Really, it's fantastic. You will use the Design Space software to view all of the Make It Now projects and to design your own creations. You can use your iPad to access the entire image library as well as all of the projects you've created on your computer. It's all right there. It's almost magical. The Design Space App would be used by unicorns if they ever wanted to get into crafting.

You can create a quick project now because of the Design Space App. You don't have to take out your laptop or clear a spot at the table for it. You can simply take out your iPad and begin working. You can use the original Explore's Bluetooth connectivity or the Explore Air's wireless technology. You can create and send your project to the computer without any cords in either case. All you have to do now is get up and press the "Cut" button. Suppose the only Cricut could create little crafting elves to do all of the tedious button pressing for us. Instead of elves, Cricut has made it simple to keep track of your project's progress. The app will display notifications on your screen when you are ready to proceed to the next step.

Many Cricut users seem to be concerned about the latest Cricut Design Space download transitioning to the offline web app.

This chapter will assuage your fears. The most frequently asked questions, as well as some troubleshooting tips, are mentioned below to help you make a smoother transfer.

The only thing you can do whether you're feeling overwhelmed or worried about this transition is to prepare yourself. Below are some responses to frequently asked questions.

Why are they going offline now?

Why did the Design Space change? That is the most pressing issue. Why should the software adjust if you are satisfied with it?

Ok, Design Space is fantastic right now online, but Cricut needs to make sure it stays that way for a long time! Moving their site to offline would enable them to improve customer functionality in ways they can't while they're reliant on content changes, web browser updates, and frameworks that might or might not accept the features they choose to implement. Also, auto-update is still an option in Design Space.

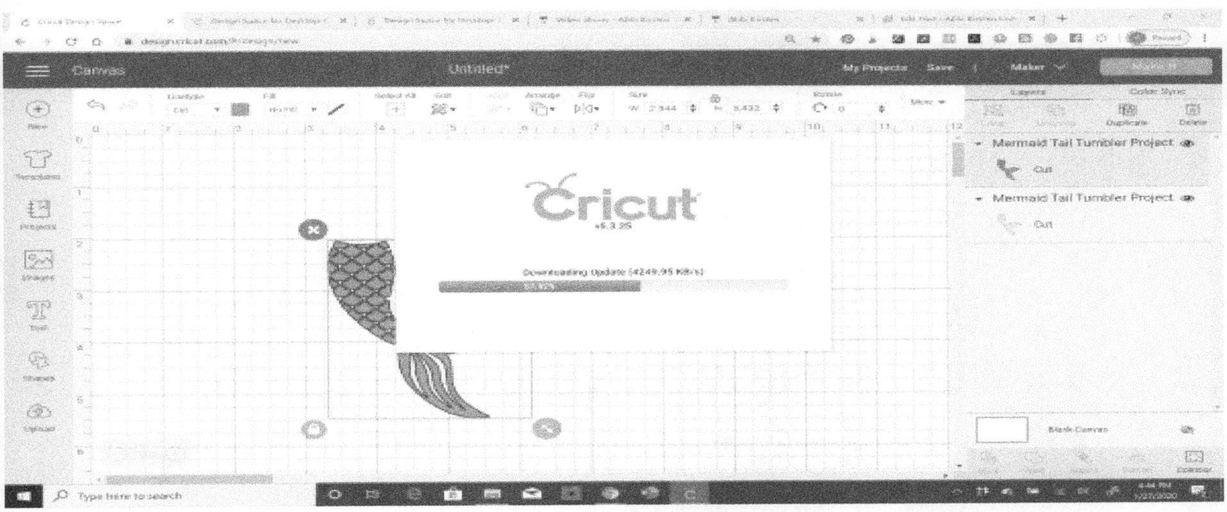

Some of you may be very cynical, and many of you are also angry right now. All will be well, and that you will be thankful for the transition in the future. Let's take a peek at a few more often asked questions regarding the latest Cricut Design Space download.

Is the latest offline app available for free?

Absolutely. The Cricut program was always free, and it will remain so in the future.

5.2 How to Install the Cricut Space Design for Desktop?

That's an excellent topic! You should download the web version right now if you haven't already. In just a few minutes, you'll get the app updated by following the instructions.

Instead of using an internet browser, you'll open Design Space on your computer once it's installed. As of January 29, 2020, going to https://www.cricut.com/design can redirect you to the web version.

5.3 Which computer is compatible with the Cricut Design Space?

Design Space is compatible with all Mac and Windows operating systems. It is incompatible with Google Chromebooks.

Users with Windows – Ensure that the program is up to date according to Windows 10 so that the latest application can be upgraded and operate smoothly.

Make sure the software is of the latest version, too, if you're a Mac user.

What happens to my application on my iPhone, iPad, or Android phone or tablet?

Absolutely nothing! Most of the Cricut users aren't aware that the mobile version has now gone offline! To put it another way, they're forcing laptop users to use the same apps as handheld mobile users.

What happens to my Cricut Access membership?

Absolutely nothing. Your Cricut subscription, as well as any images you've purchased, will be migrated to the latest software automatically. You don't have to do something – it's as easy as that.

What's the deal with my app being too slow? What's the deal about the app not loading at all?

It's understandable that if anything isn't effective for you, you'll get frustrated. But there is good news: you can get help!

If you're having problems with your program not loading or working slowly, the first you can do is ensure you do have the most recent update of software installed on your Mac or Windows device. This is the issue for 99 percent of citizens, and it is easily fixed.

If you've already upgraded your program and yet experiencing problems, uninstalling and reinstalling the software is suggested until your machine has been updated.

You can also make sure that your hard drive has at least 2GB of free space.

5.4 What if I've done it all?

If you verified all of the things mentioned above, please make contact with Cricut Member Care. They are fantastic at assisting!

They still have a support bubble on the lower left side of the latest web app. This allows you to quickly communicate your problem by choosing a topic, group, and even drawing on the screen to highlight unique issues!

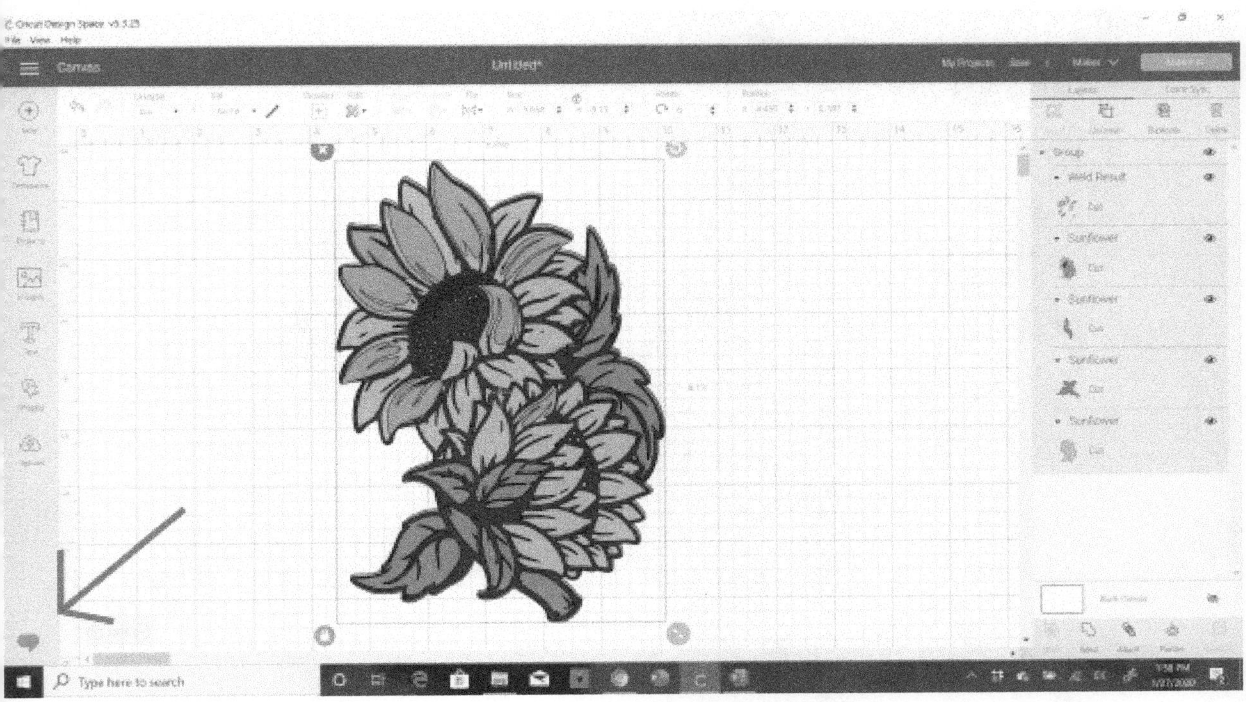

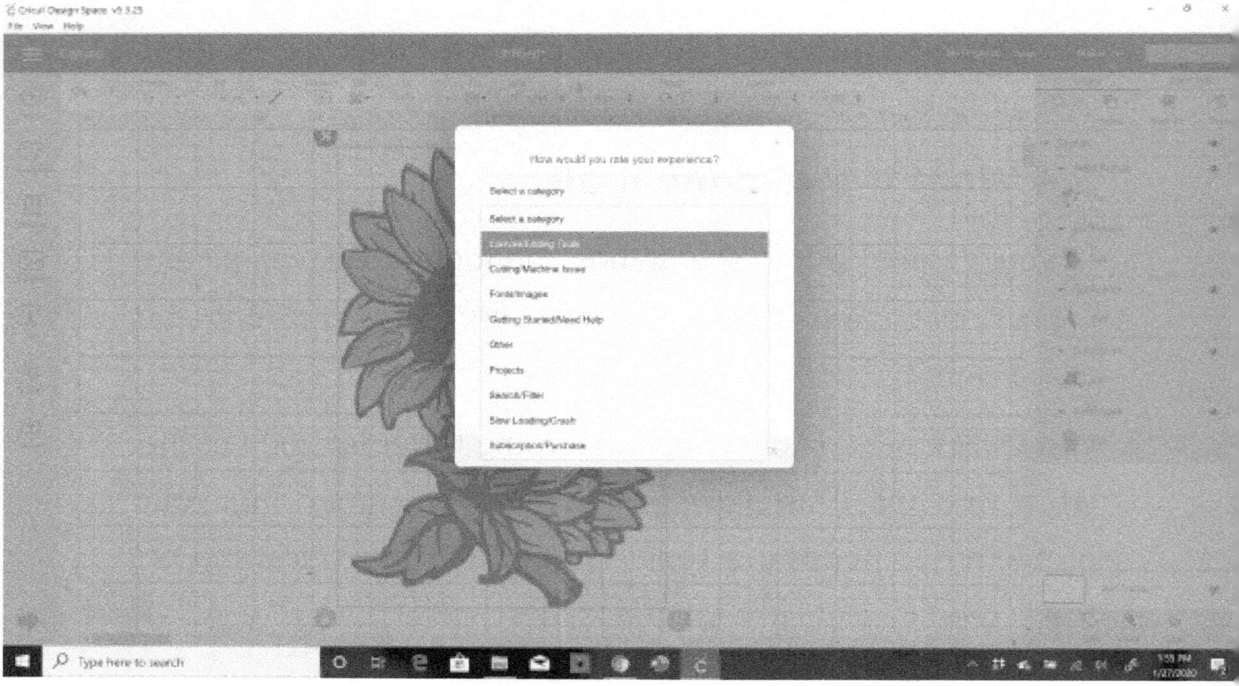
How would you rate your experience?
Select a category
Select a category
Cutting/Machine Issues
Fonts/Images
Getting Started/Need Help
Other
Projects
Search/Filter
Slow Loading/Crash
Subscription/Purchase
Type here to search

How can I discuss my Design Space projects with others?

In the same manner as before! The sharing alternative is still accessible, but the Link would open in the web app rather than online.

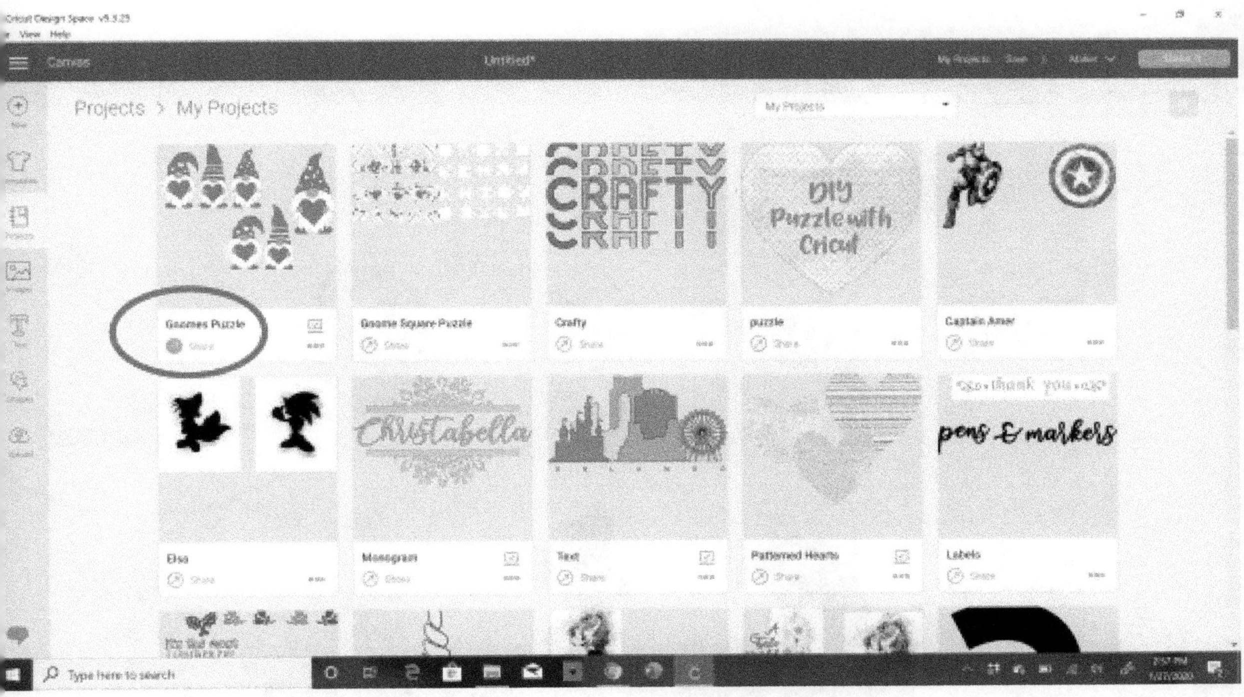

5.5 How can I get Image Files to Use Offline?

Pick a picture and press download in the left-hand corner if you choose to use it while you aren't wired to the internet. You can modify, load and cut the picture without having to use the internet until it has been effectively saved for offline use!

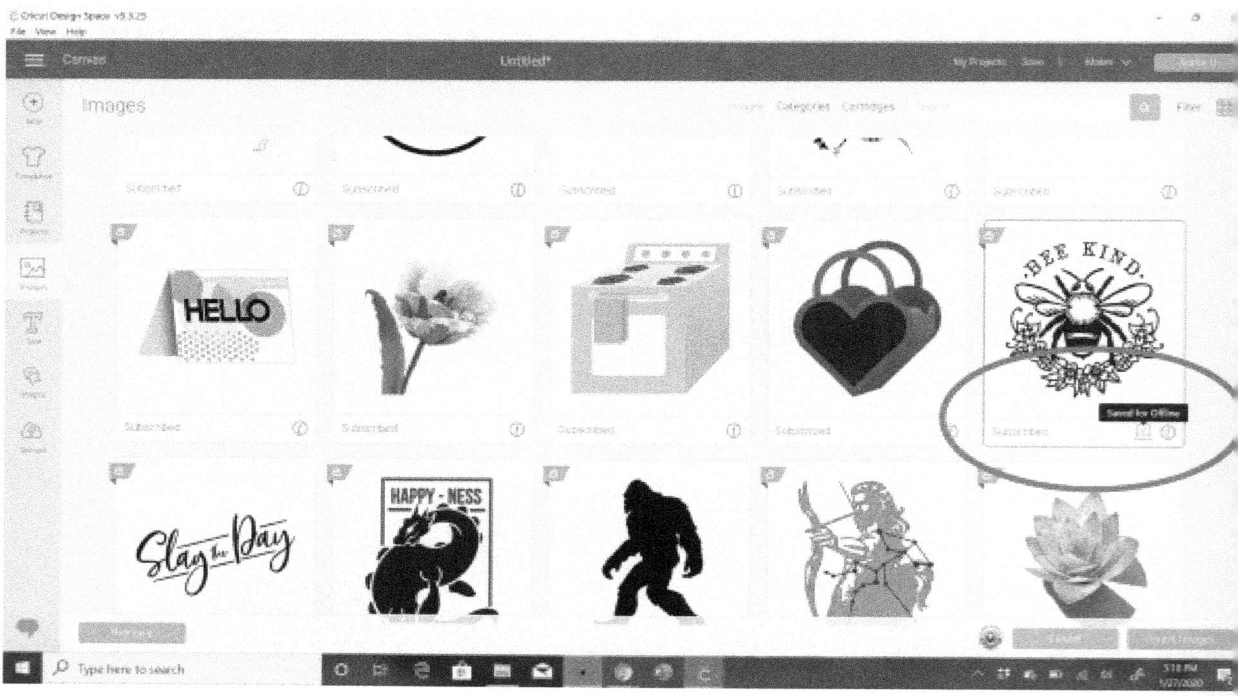

When I open the window, my screen is black.

You can fix this by clearing the cache and reopening the application, according to Cricut.

Design Space is sluggish.

If this happens, Cricut recommends doing a "force-reload." Click View > force-reload to do so.

I'm unable to see any of my tasks or images

If photos seem absent, close the software and reopen it after ensuring that your internet link is operational. The internet is also expected to load photos downloaded from the cloud before they are saved for offline use. Keep in mind to watch this tutorial to learn how to save your creations and photographs for offline use!

For now, that's all there is to the latest Design Space computer experience!

Chapter 6: Cricut Projects

If you own a Cricut, you are well aware of the wide range of options available. Cricut Print Then Cut is one of the best features. It makes using a Cricut much more flexible by allowing you to cut custom images created outside of Design Space.

6.1 DIY Wood Burned Ornaments Cricut Craft

What You'll Need

- Wood Slices
- Heat Gun
- Scorch Marker
- Heat Protector Mat
- Transfer Tape
- Removable Vinyl or Stencil
- Brush and Mod Podge
- Cutting machine (use a Cricut)
- Hot Glue Gun and Ribbon
- SVG Cut Files

The Scorch Marker is truly incredible. You put the marker where you intend to make the wood-burning and by using a heat gun to change the color to a wood-burnt look. You can use a heat gun to try to warm it up. But don't use a hairdryer or heat press as both of these have failed miserably.

6.2 Wood Burned Ornament: A Step-by-Step Guide

Step 1: Making a stencil

You might skip this move if you're decent at freehand. To make ornaments look nice, used the Cricut for cutting stencil vinyl.

You are free to design ornaments of your own or whatever you like with SVG cut images.

Except for these, which are on the top of the list of SVG during twelve Days of Christmas, all are described in alphabetical order. "Jesus is the Reason," The nativity scene, and Merry Christmas are the themes mostly used.

The designs will be larger and illuminated when you import them into the design applications, such as Cricut Design Room. For guidance on how to upload files and photographs to design a room, read chapter five of this book.

The first step is to adjust the color of all the prototypes to a single color. About the fact that the stencil vinyl used is blue, you can also go for black. It doesn't matter what color they are, but they all should be of the same color.

Then, on the lower right of the design, use the arrow button to shrink the icons to suit an ornament. Ornaments of Wood slice are averaged 2.5-3′′ in diameter, so you should stay inside that size.

When you've scaled it, make sure to press the connect button in the layers menu's bottom right corner to ensure that the template is cut precisely as it seems to you. Or Else, Cricut would want to cram all into as little room as possible. You're now going to press the 'make it' icon.

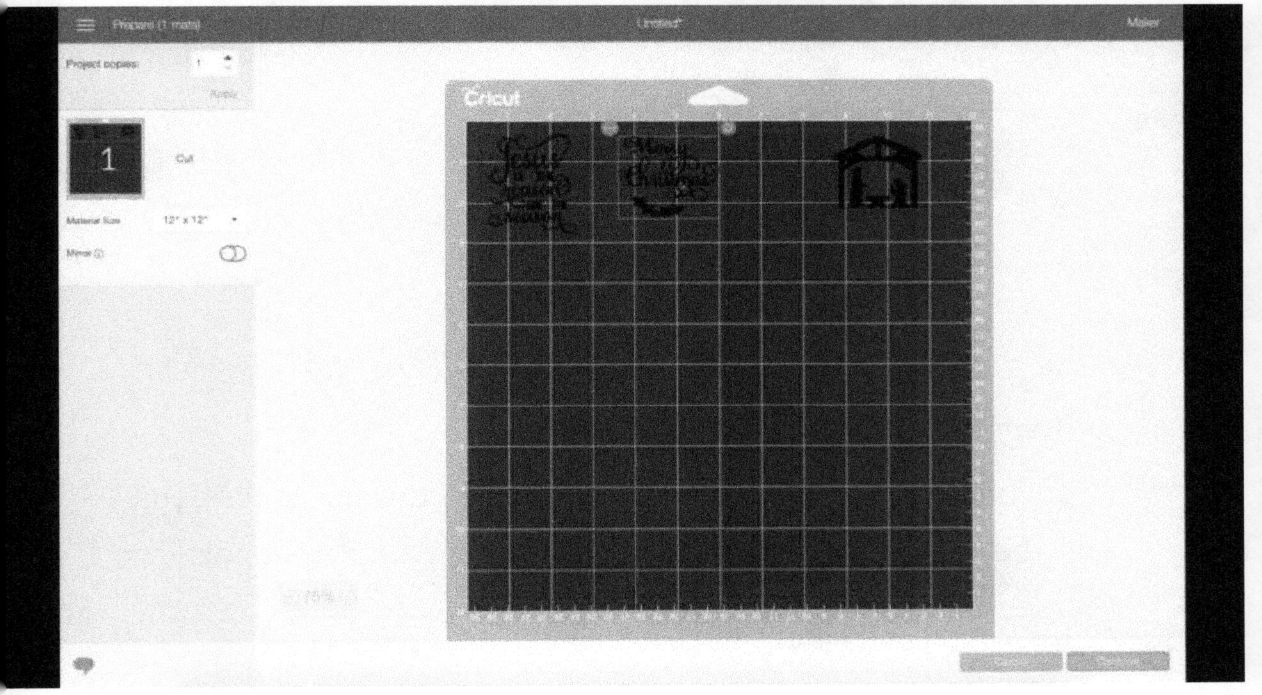

When you've arrived at the screen of the mat, press on the designs and drag them apart a little. Since we're producing stencils, they won't fit if they're too near together.

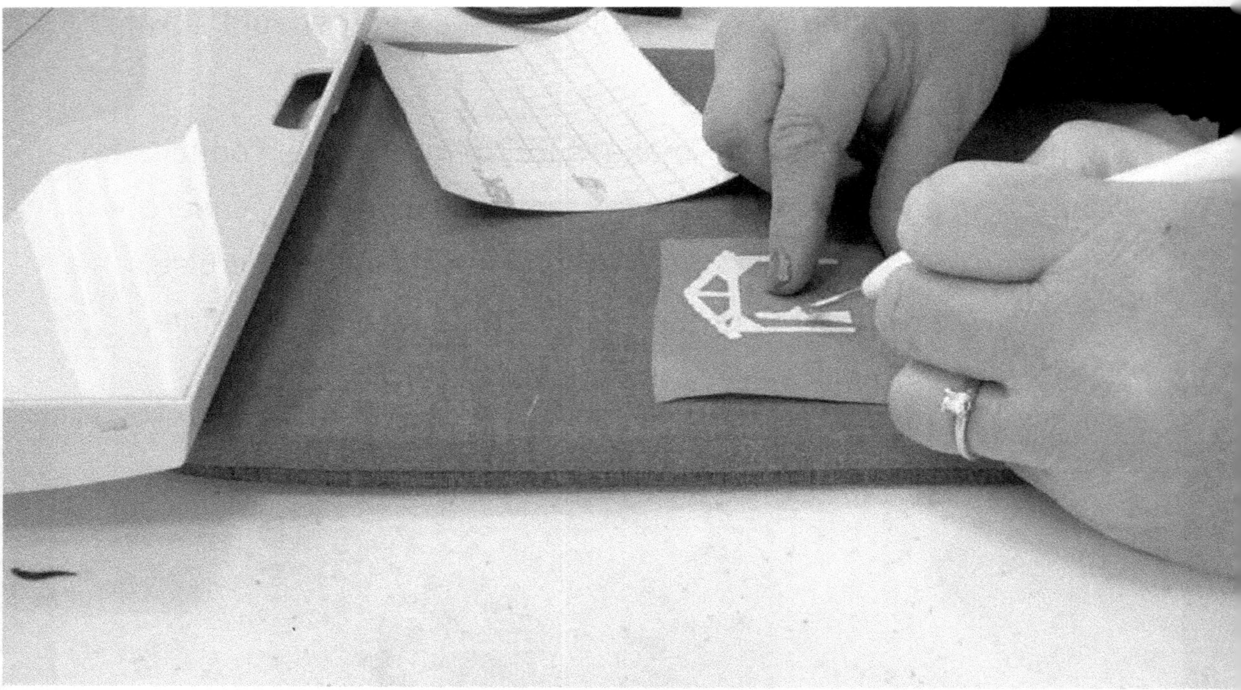

The designs were cut on Oracle Stencil Film, which can be purchased directly from Amazon.

You'll eradicate the center and abandon the outer portions of the vinyl while producing stencils. Weeding labels or jersey patterns is the inverse of this.

Step 2: Transferring the Stencil

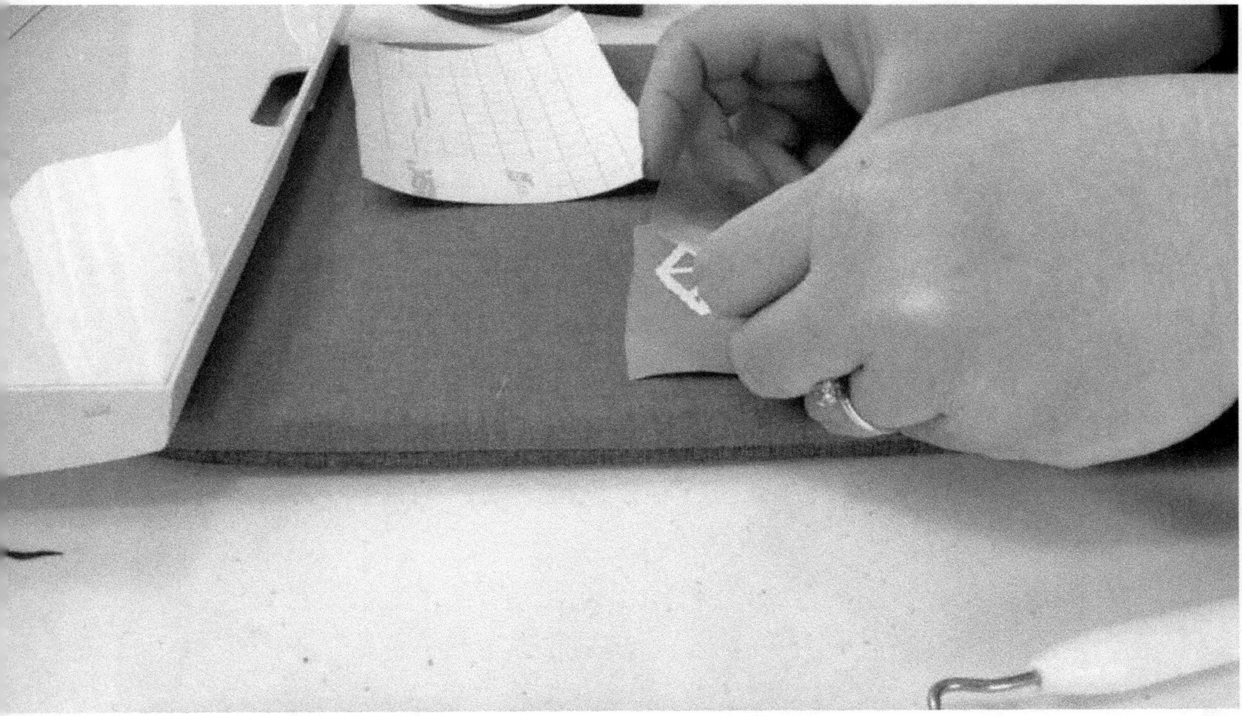

Place the transfer paper onto the Stencil so you can shift it to the ornaments of wood slice after all of the parts have been weeded out. Use plain contact paper for transfer tape, which can be found in most stores such as Walmart.

Smoothly move the paper down with the scraper tool to ensure it adheres to all the vinyl.

Get rid of the backing from the vinyl stencil and put it on the wood-slice decoration. Take all the time you need aligning the Stencil; as far as you don't press it flat, you'll be free to pass it around to the middle.

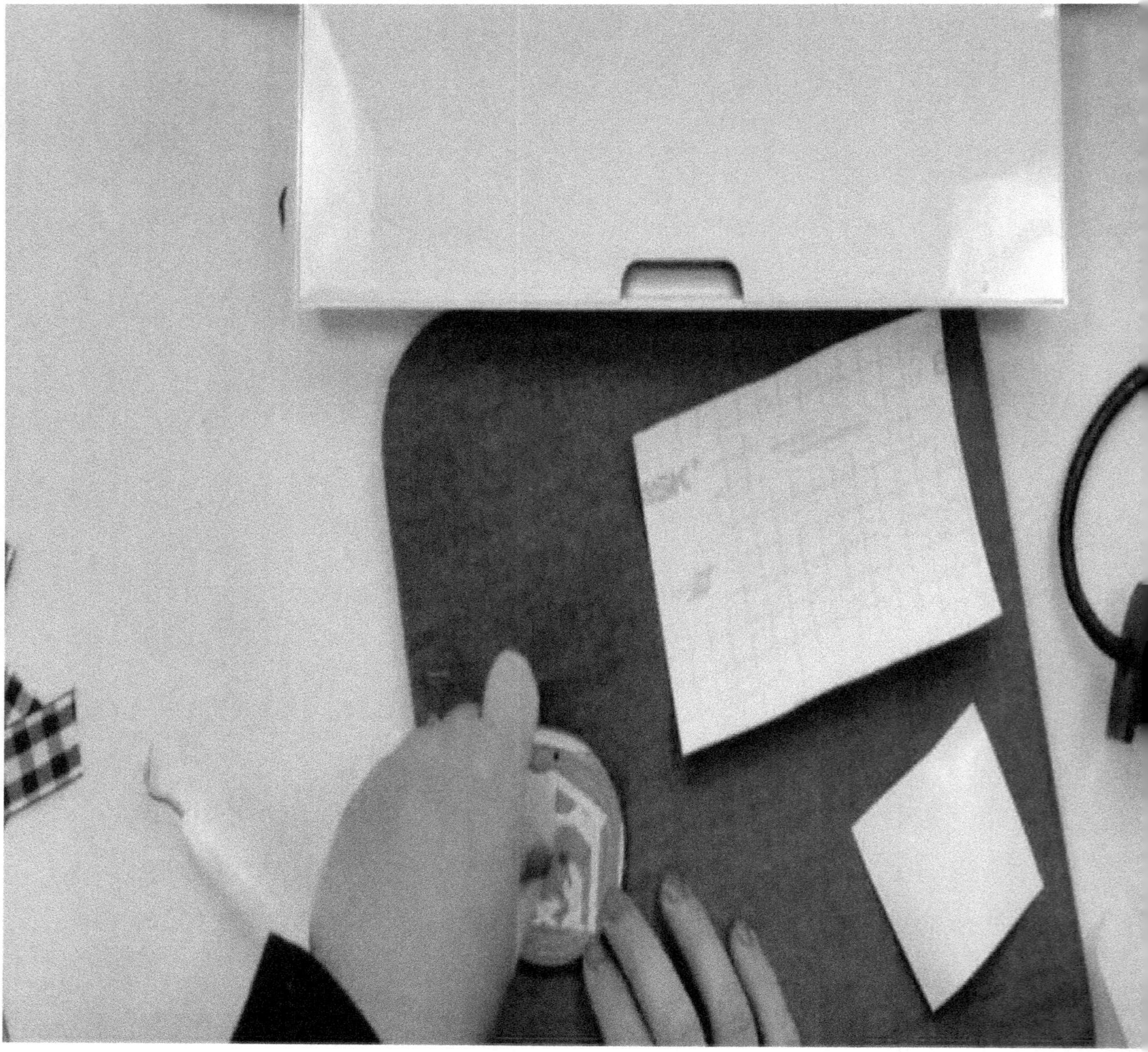

Using the scraper tool to stick the Stencil to the wood slice until you've got the design centered. Take the transition document away from you gently now. Be certain that all of the stencil bits adhere to the wood.

For any bits, try to unstick with the transfer tape; simply re-scrape and set it down again.

Use the scorch marker until all of the stencils are in place.

Jesus
IS THE
reason
season
Merry

Step 3: Filling the Stencil with the Scorch Marker

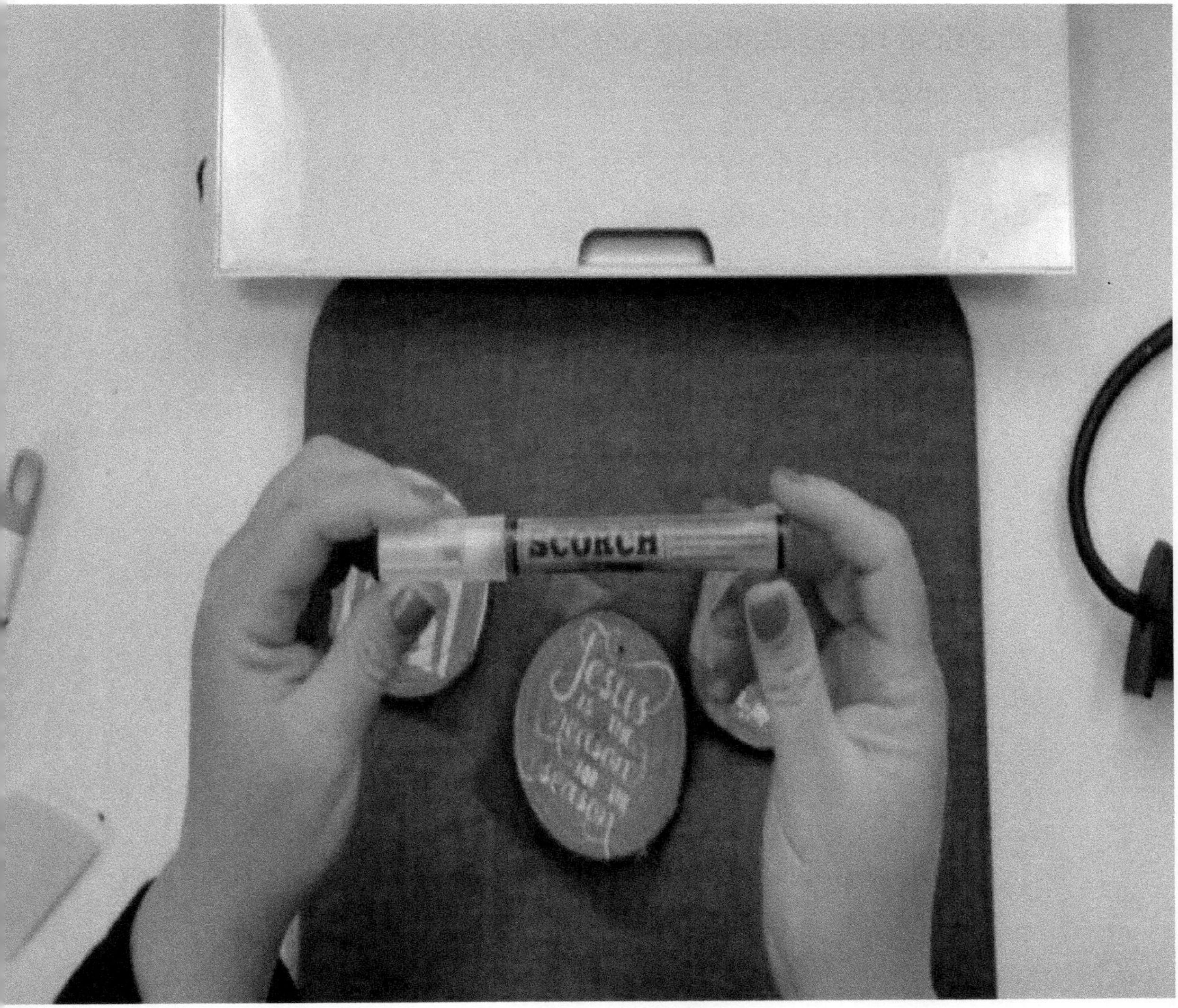

When using the scorch marker for the first time, give it a good shake. And take a scrap of paper and use it in priming the marker. You can choose to include the backs of your ornaments.

However, you'll need a place to repeatedly force down the marker's tip. It can take a long time to prime the market for the first time. Continue until the liquid comes out of the marker's edge.

Start to fill in all open areas of the Stencil with the marker after it has been prepared.

If the marker is well primed, the wood can shift color almost automatically. You might need to again prime the marker when you go if you're making a tonne of ornaments. Strip the wood slice ornament with stencils until you've finished coloring on all of the ornaments with the scorch pen.

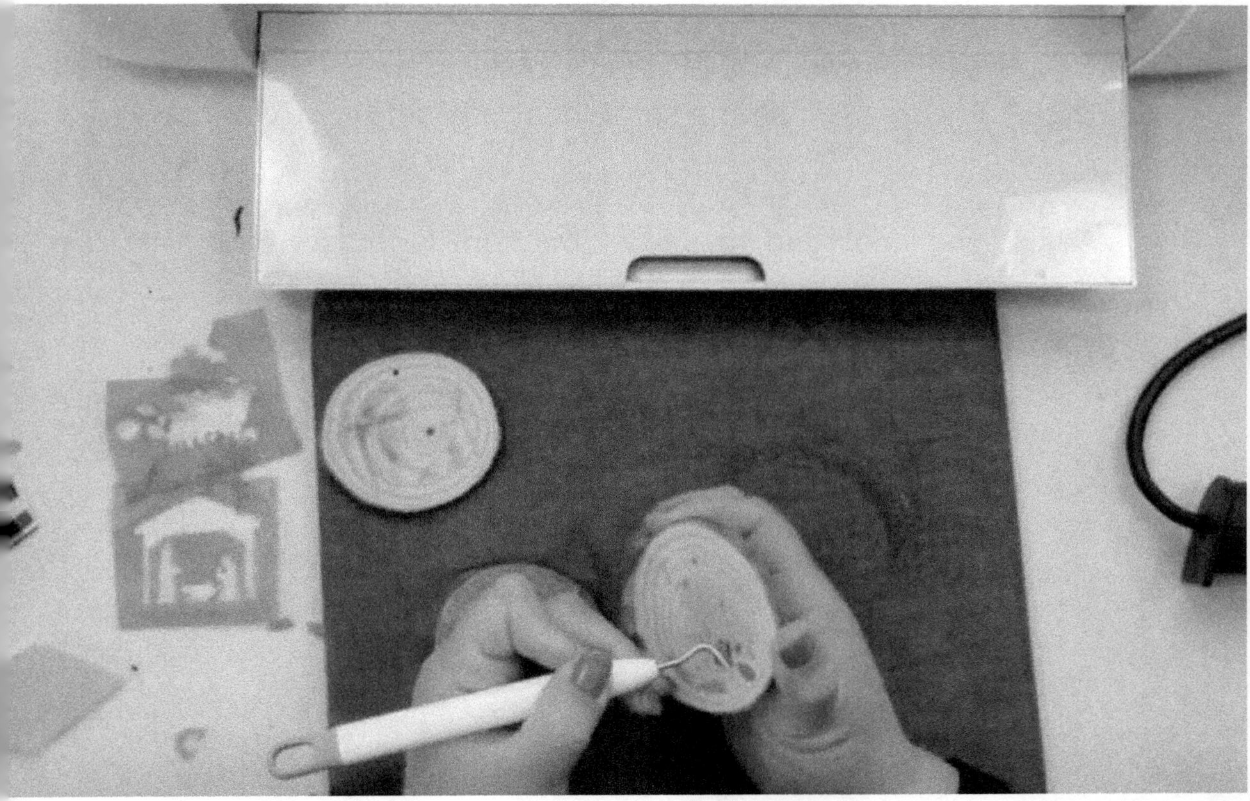

You might need to use your weeding method to remove the stencil pieces. You can also check where you used the marker.

You can use a heat gun now to really get it out.

Step 4: Using a Heat Gun, apply heat

For a moment, let's talk of the heat gun. This stuff gets wet, hot enough to bubble in the finishing off the table. Heat up the silicone chairs.

You can use a heat shield pad to cover your table if you do this. You can also use the same heat pressing mat you used for tops.

Adjust the heat gun to low or medium-high and switch it about as you would a hairdryer while drying your hair.

You'll see the picture darkening when the wood-slice ornaments heat up. It can take a few minutes after adding heat to show the full effect.

Allow the ornaments to cool before handling them. They'll be nice and cozy.

Step 5: Use Mod Podge or another sealant to seal the project.

I'm not sure if the sealer's purpose is to shield your ornament or to pop the wood-burned image. It makes a huge improvement in the appearance of your ornament.

So don't forget to use the sealer. Applying Mod Podge to the surface will perform the job perfectly.

Step 6: Add Bows and Ribbons

Attach a string or a bit of twine to mount the decoration once the sealer has dried. And, to top it off, you can hot glued on bows or any other embellishments you like.

You can create your own forms of the Hulk, Captain America, Batman, Spiderman, Ironman, and Donatello, the Ninja Turtle, after scouring the Cricut Design Space Library for all the required design elements. These masks are simple to put on and take off, and they cover enough of the face!

These DIY Superhero Masks came together quickly and easily thanks to a few factors. First, use your Cricut Maker to cut out all of the various bits, so you don't have to do all of the careful cutting with your hand. Second, use Cricut's brand new Easy Press Mini to put them together, which made adding all the tiny information a breeze!

The Cricut Easy Press Mini

Cricut's Easy Press Mini is the latest member of the Easy Press family. It has the same heat plate and dries as the larger heat presses, but it's much smaller and has a precision top. It has 3 separate heat levels and a heat-proof foundation and measures just 3.4 x 2.1''. It's lightweight, simple to use, and perfect for small, informative projects!

cricut
cricut

When you should use a larger heat press to add these little iron-on specifics, the EasyPress Mini can help you to operate in tight spaces, ensuring that each tiny part was completely stable. The Mini is also great for circular things (like hats, shoes, bows) and patterns in or near seams and pockets, in addition to minor cuts like the ones used here.

One of the favorite aspects of occupied with the Easy Press Mini is how much smoother layering iron-on bits is! Instead of trying to shield the lowest layers from contact with a bigger heat press or overheating previous layers, the Easy Press Mini can help you to get into tiny spaces and heat just the parts that you want!

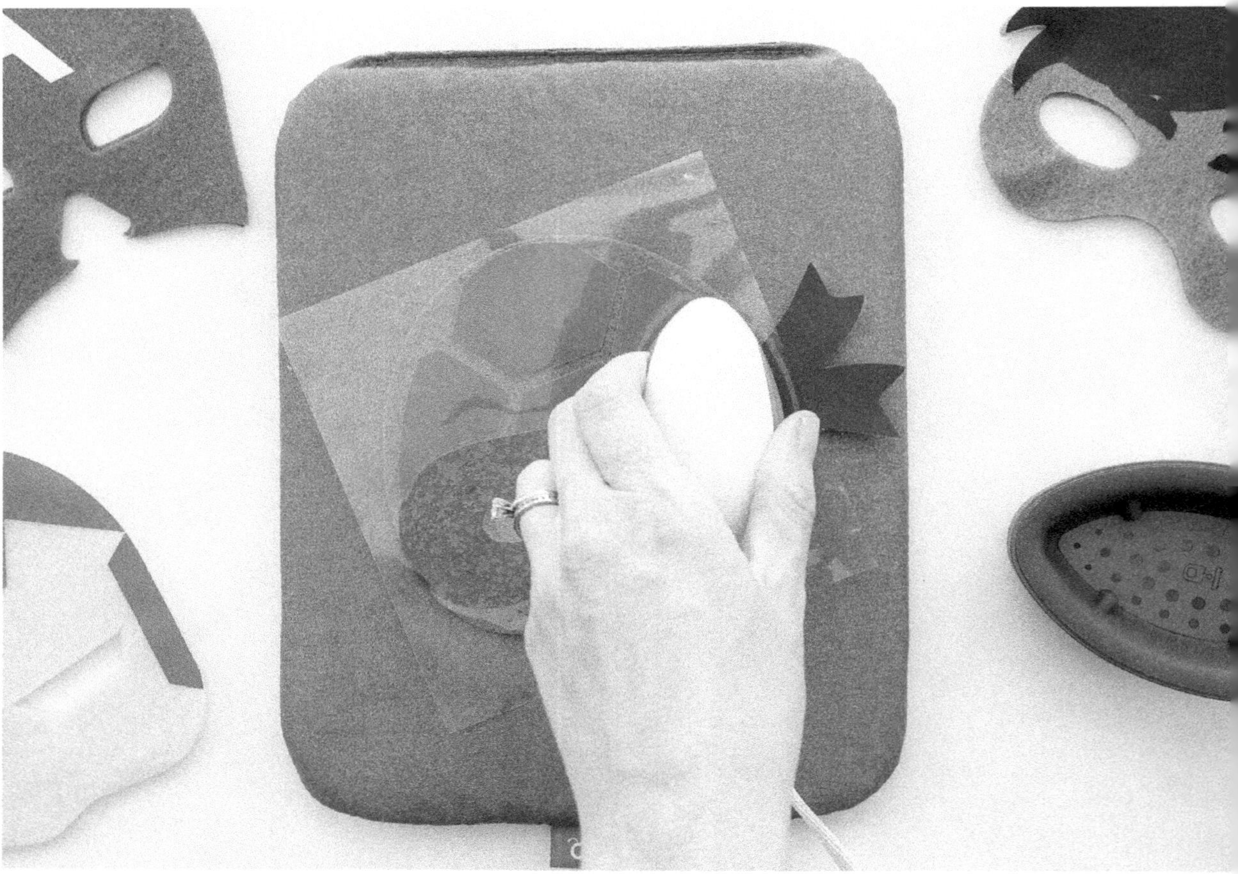

Supplies Needed

These masks are incredibly easy to create and take just minutes to put together. Here's what you'll require:

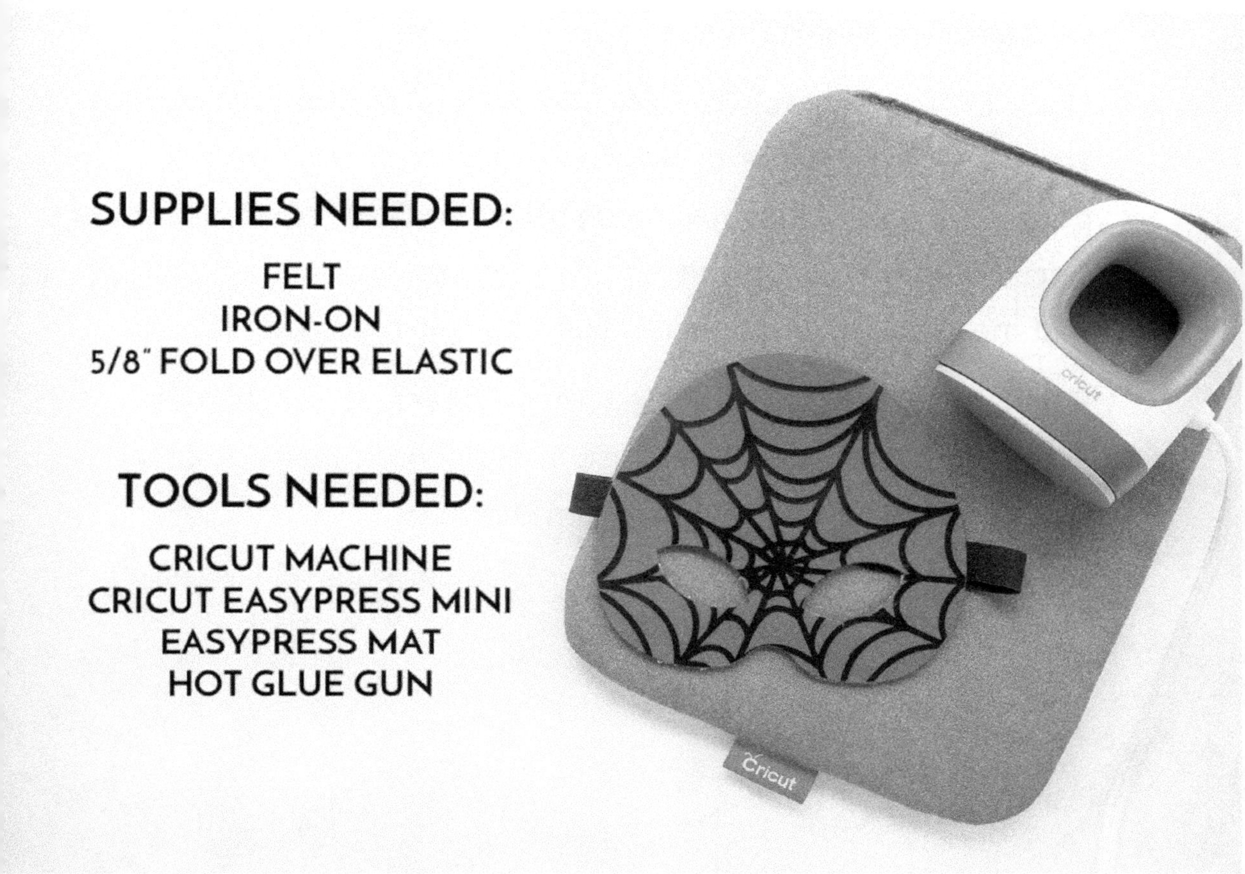

- Cricut Maker
- Easy Press Mini
- Hot Glue Gun
- Easy Press Mat
- Iron-On Vinyl
- Felt
- Fold-Over Elastic

Cutting Out Mask Pieces

Many of the "decorative" features are crafted from iron-on vinyl and fixed to the front of the masks, which are made up of 2 layers of felt fused together. You'll need to use a Cricut machine to cut out all of the parts until you've built and measured your masks to suit your girl.

Begin by cutting out two felt mask bases for each mask you're creating. When you use the Cricut Maker's Rotary Blade, you'll get perfect cuts from the felt!

Then, using iron-on vinyl, cut out all of the mask specifics. Make sure the "Mirror" button on the cut screen is chosen, and then pick out all the bad aspects of the logo until they can be attached to the masks.

6.3 Iron On Mask Details

You'll want to apply all of the iron-on information to the upper layer before mounting the masks. You'll want to link to the cooperating Cricut Easy Press Heat Guide while operating with every Cricut EasyPress to ensure you're using the correct settings. It urges you to set your EasyPress Mini to the Low setting by choosing the Easy Press Mini, felt as the base coat, and iron-on as the heat-transfer content. The felt mask should be Pre-heat for around 5 seconds until the EasyPress Mini is hot.

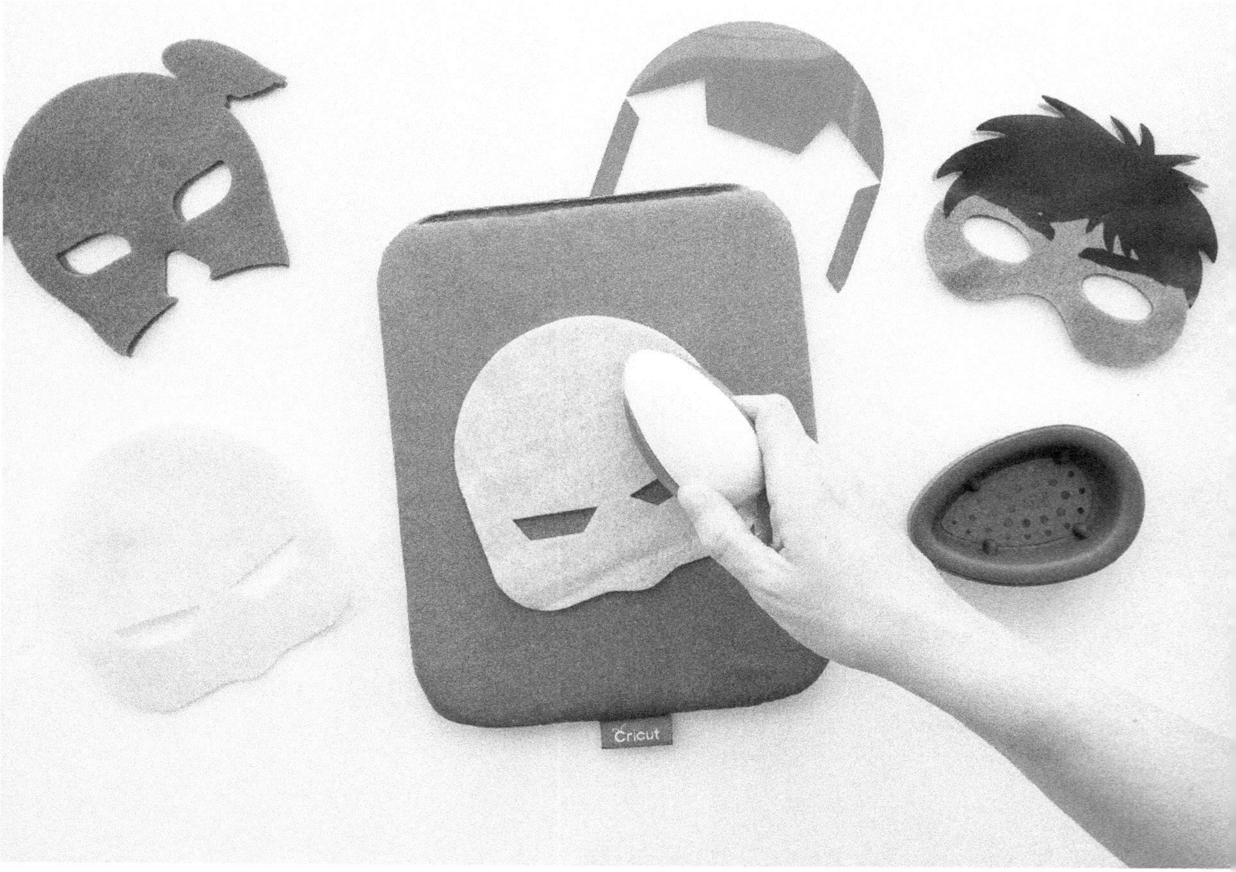

Then, iron the iron-on information on topmost of the mask for around 30 seconds while rotating the Easy Press Mini with a gentle touch. Remove the transparent transfer layer until iron-on materials and the mask have properly cooled. Continue to apply iron-on detailing to the front mask before it is over.

Assembling The Mask

Once you've finished the front mask, it's time to put it together! Place the two mask bits, right sides down, onto your work surface.

Begin by applying a very narrow line of hot glue to the opposite side of the lower layer over one eye. Until the adhesive sets, lock the top sheet, right-side-up, to ensure that the eye holes are correctly aligned. Rep on the opposite eye.

Safe the elastic after the eyes have been taped shut. On one line, glue one corner of the fold-over elastic to one side and then the other. Check that the elastic is not bent and that it is long enough to go around your child's head.

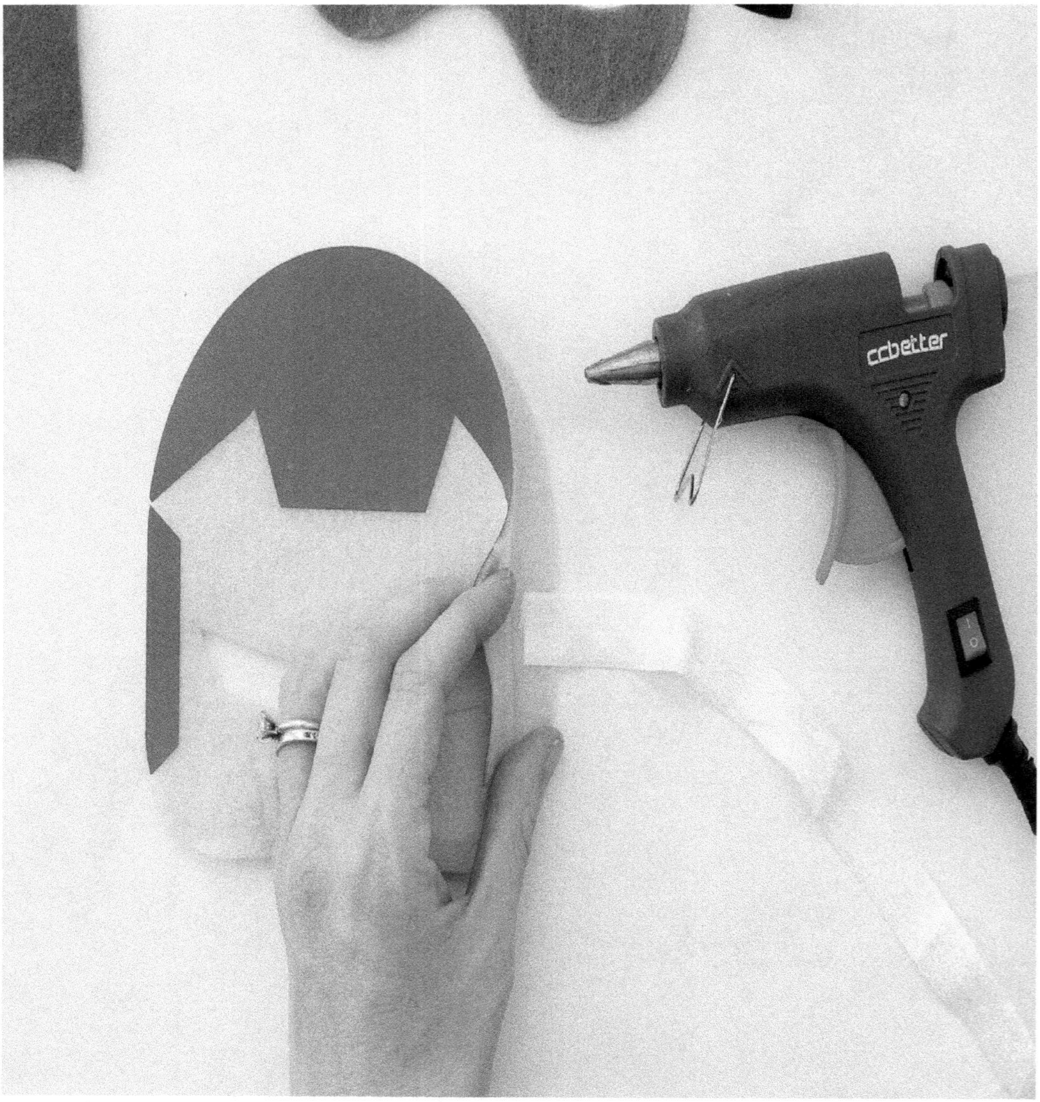

NOTE: Start with at least 11 inches of elastic and incorporate more if required!

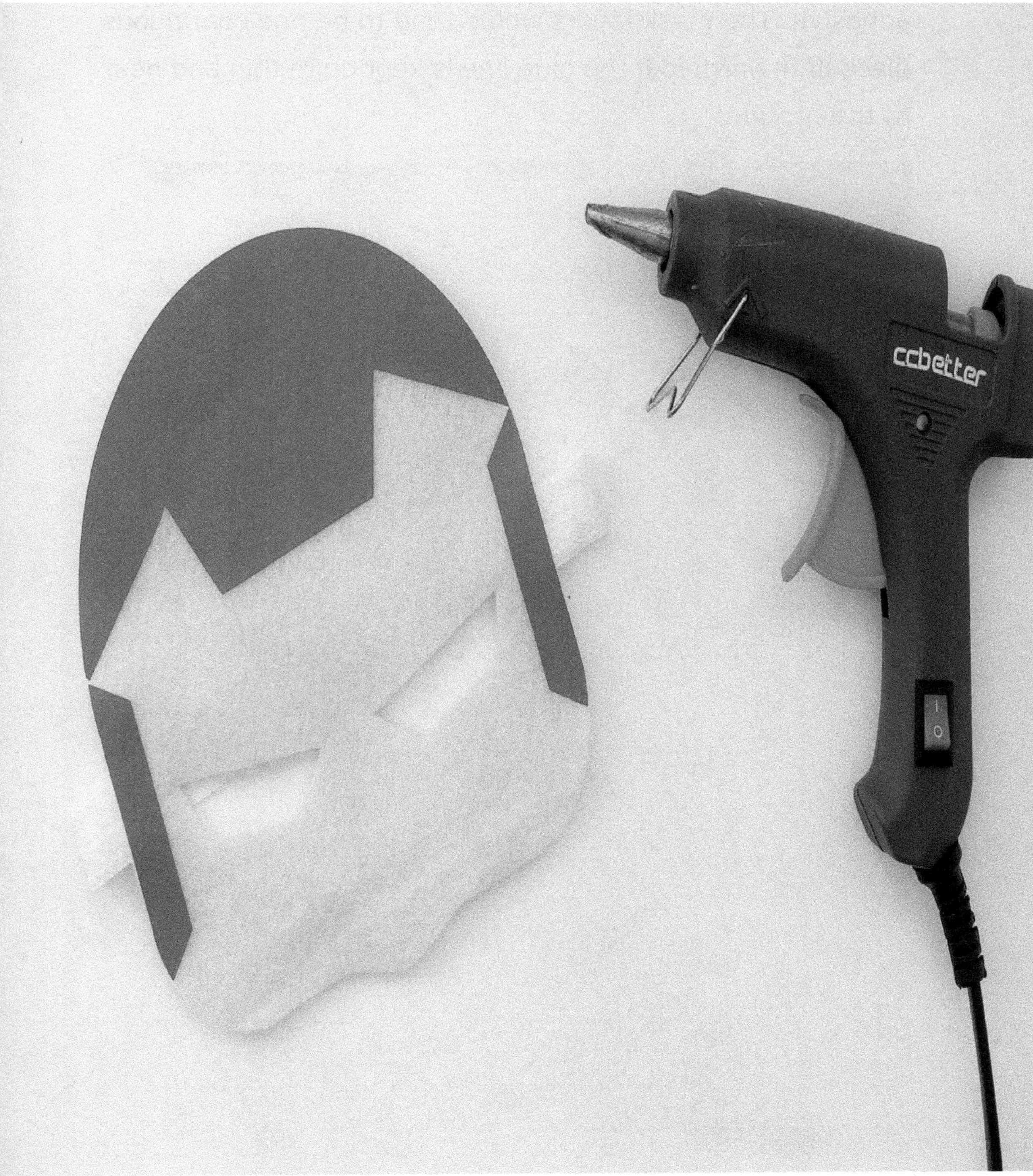
ccbetter

The final move is to join the 2 layers across the edge with adhesive. The mask layers would tend to be one continuous piece until finished if the glue line is kept quite thin and near to the ground!

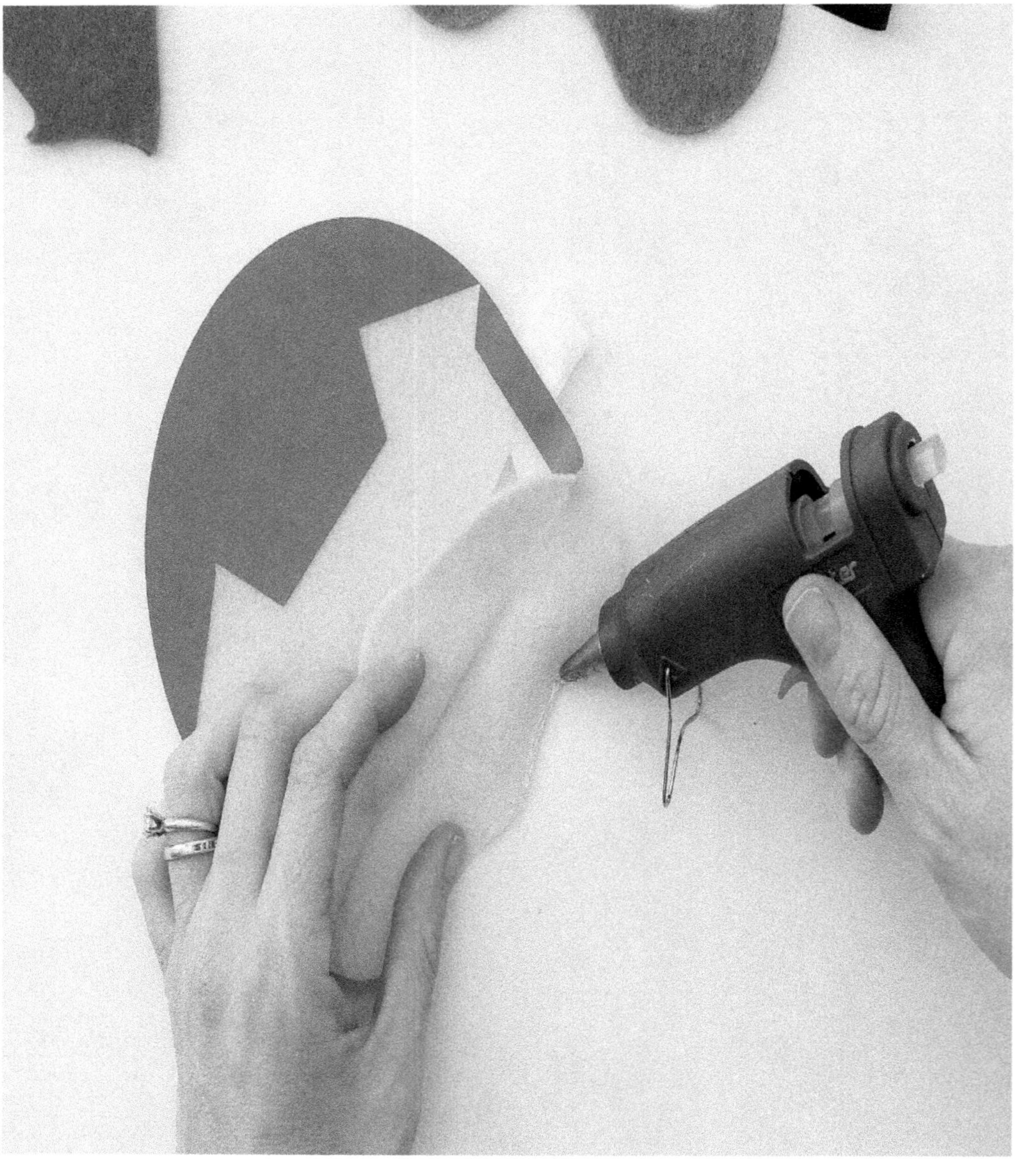

After you've finished one mask, repeat with as many superheroes as you like! Then make a few more because they're so simple and enjoyable!

Finally, give them to the children and let their dreams run wild!

While you have the time of dressing all year in your homes, these masks will make perfect Halloween costumes. These are perfect for little children and babies that don't want anything on their appearances because of their tiny size, fluffy felt, and stretchy elastic. If you're short of time, their easy-and-quick assembly can help you throw together costumes in no time (particularly if you match the masks with these twenty-minute capes!).

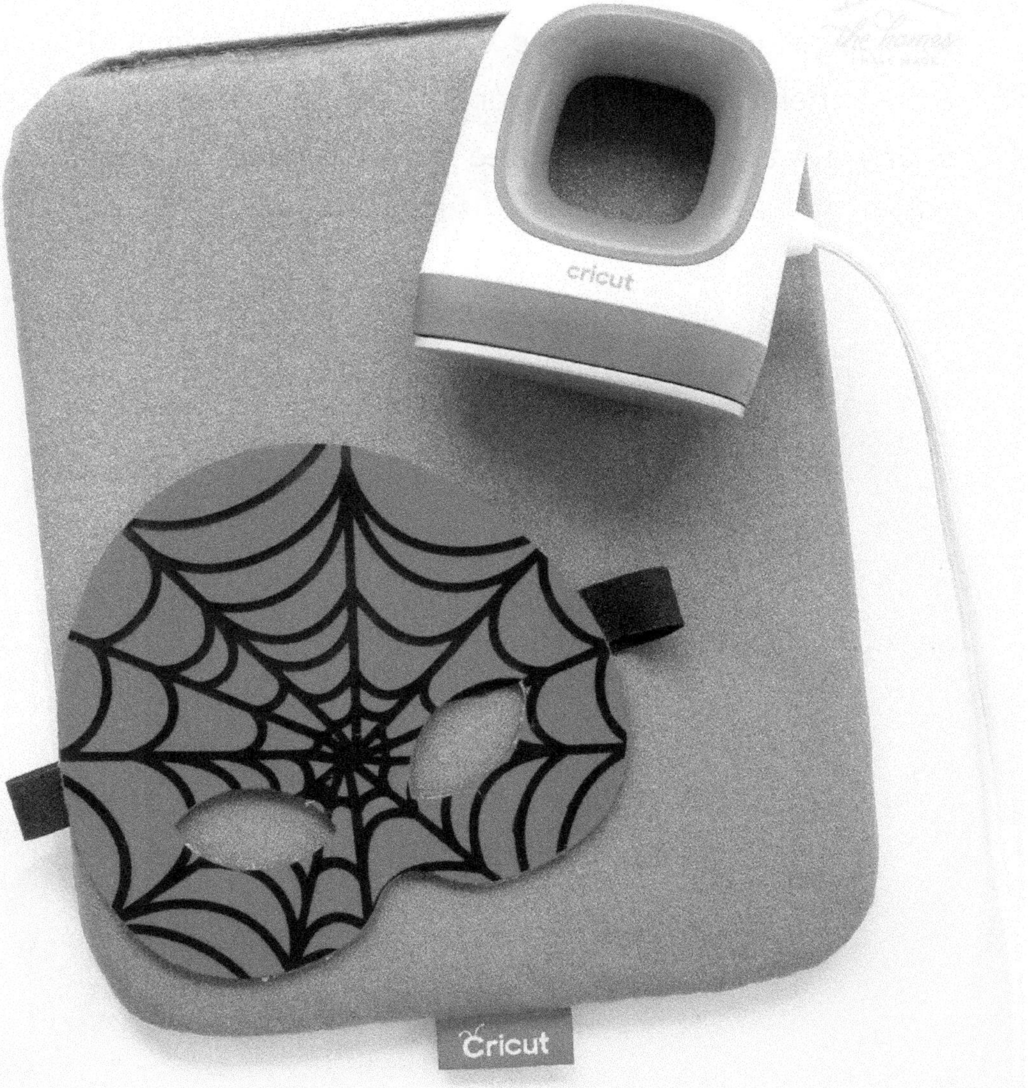

DO-IT-YOURSELF

SUPER HERO MASKS

WITH THE CRICUT EASYPRESS MINI

These DIY Superhero Masks are a lot of fun to create, and using the Cricut Easy Press Mini eliminates a great deal of the frustration that comes with iron-on creations. If you create them for Halloween or just for fun, they'll be worth your time and will guarantee big ol' smiles on your kids' faces!

Chapter 7: Cricut Project Ideas

There are about as many Cricut ideas as there are humans, multiplied by the materials available. You can make great DIY crafts for every purpose with a Cricut Maker, Cricut Explore, or the adorable Cricut Joy.

Let's have a look at several projects that range from simple to difficult.

7.1. Tassels

Tassels may be used in a variety of ways. These are extremely simple to produce and can be made to fit any task. Use them as a keyring or zipper pick, add them to the sides of pillows or covers, hang them from a rope to create a banner, and a thousand other items! You may even make them out of leather or faux leather for a more elegant look. Tassels look great on almost everything.

someone
smiles today
REMEMBER THIS

Materials

- Fabric mat
- 12" x 18" fabric rectangles
- Glue gun
- Cricut machine

Instructions

- Launch Design Space to begin a new design.
- Click the "Image" icon in the bottom left-hand corner and type "tassel" into the search box.
- Press "Insert" after selecting the illustration of a rectangle with lines on either side.
- Arrange fabric on the mat and use the Cricut to cut out the pattern.
- Take the fabric off the mat and save the excess square.
- Beginning from the uncut side, position the material face down and roll tightly. As required, untangle the fringe.
- To attach the tassel at the top, use some waste fabric and a hot glue stick.
- Use your beautiful tassels to decorate anything you like!

7.2. Paw Print Socks

Socks are the epitome of comfort. Small paw prints add a cool, secret decoration to the base of your socks. Every time you cuddle up, show off your affection towards pets. You can do this with about every small style or even add text to the base of your foot to add a quotation. You can select any kind of socks you choose. Please ensure the sock and vinyl colors contrast for easy reading. Or, for a hidden design, make them all in the same color! Under certain lighting, the vinyl shine will contrast with the fabric. You'll require your Cricut EasyPress or iron for this since it uses heat transfer vinyl.

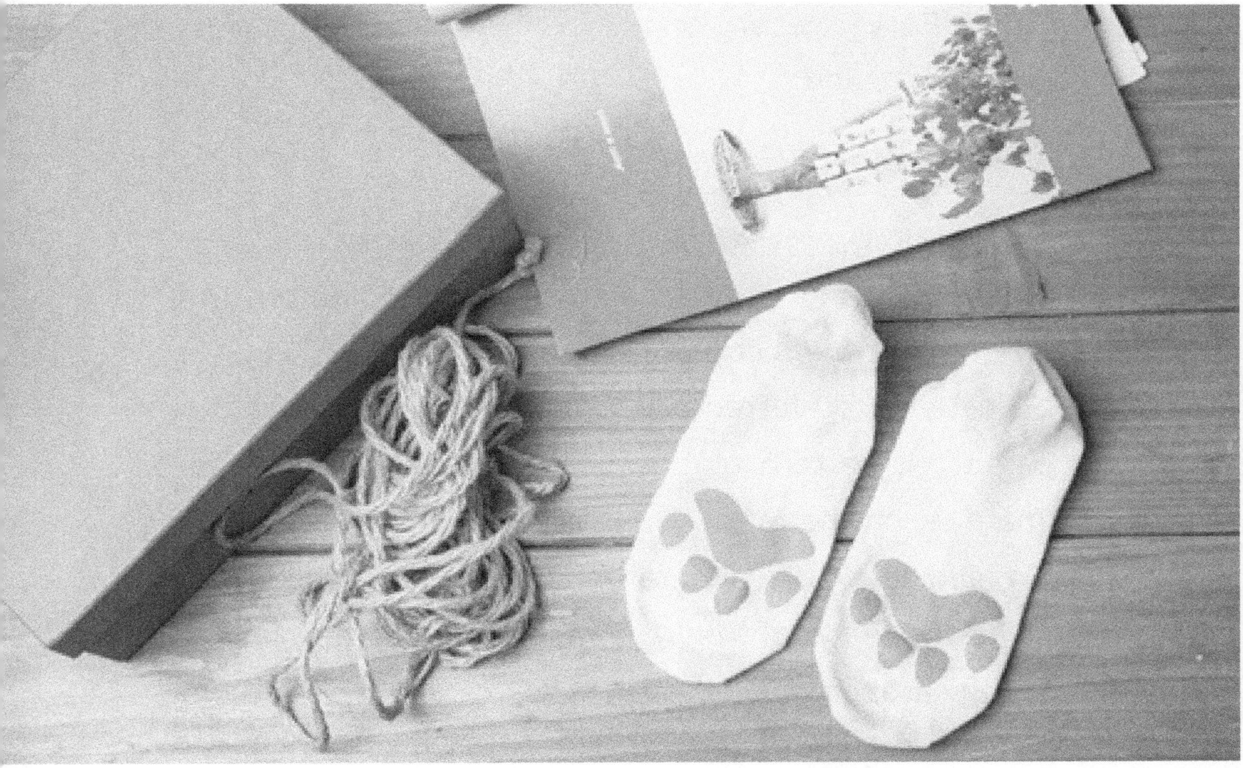

Materials

- Socks
- Weeding tool or pick
- Scrap cardboard
- Heat transfer vinyl
- Cutting mat
- Cricut EasyPress or iron
- Cricut machine

Instructions

- Build a new project in Cricut Design Space.
- Check for "paw prints" using the "Photo" button in the bottom left-hand corner.
- Select your preferred paw prints and click "Insert."
- Send the pattern to the Cricut by placing the iron-on material on the mat.
- To eliminate excess material, use a pick or weeding tool.
- Take the material from the mat and stuff the socks with scrap cardboard.
- Put the iron-on material onto the socks' bottoms.
- To attach it to the iron-on material, use EasyPress.
- Take the cardboard from the socks after they have cooled.
- Put on your adorable paw print socks!

7.3. Monogrammed Drawstring Bag

Drawstring bags are simple to use and carry. They're just as easy to produce as they are to use! These bags can be kept on hand for anyone in your family to pick and go as required. You may use monograms to distinguish them, or you can use a different pattern on each one to modify it for a certain purpose or simply to decorate it. This can also be used as gift bags! The designs are made of heat transfer vinyl, so you'll need your Cricut EasyPress or iron for this project.

Hair
stuff

Materials

- Heat transfer vinyl
- Two matching rectangles of fabric
- Weeding tool or pick
- Cutting mat
- Needle and thread
- Ribbon
- Cricut machine
- Cricut EasyPress or iron

Instructions

- Build a new project in Cricut Design Space.
- Check for "monogram" using the "Image" icon in the bottom left-hand corner.
- Select the monogram you want to use and press "Insert."
- Place the shiny liner side of the iron-on material on the mat and give the pattern to the Cricut.
- To eliminate excess material, use the weeding tool or a pick.
- Remove the monogram out of the mat.
- The monogram should be centered on your material and moved down a couple of inches, so it doesn't get rolled up as the ribbon is created.
- The pattern should be ironed onto the fabric.
- Put the two rectangles along such that the fabric's outside side is faced inward.

- Leave a seam allowance when you sew along with the corners. Let the top open and stop it a few inches below the top.
- Fold the bag's top back until the stitches are reached.
- Sew around the folded edge's bottom, keeping the sides open.
- Turn bag's right side out.
- The ribbon should be threaded through the loop at the top of the bag.
- Bring what you need in your fresh drawstring pocket!

7.4. Customized Pillow

A simple concept that is often requested and quick to personalize. Make the pillow of your dreams!

STEWART
EST. 1998

Materials

- Insert Cricut Access
- Protective Sheet Pillow Cover
- Glitter Iron-On Vinyl
- Iron-On
- Cricut Easypress Mat
- Cricut Machine

Instructions

- From the Home tab of the Cricut Design Space, select "New Project."
- Click the text icon in the lower right corner of the page and choose the font you like. Fill in your name and adjust the size of the box corner to fit your pillow.
- To add an additional bit of text for your Est. Year, choose the Text button. Drag and arrange your last name properly.
- Choose all textboxes at the same time and hit the attach button. It will link the two text boxes, allowing for precise cutting.
- The screen appears as you click the "Make It" icon. Allow that the Mirror is turned on.
- To switch on and off the mirror setting, click the image in the upper left corner. The image above appears on the computer. Turn the "off" switch on.

- Press the Mirror button; the mat will now reflect your mirrored image, and you're ready to load your Iron-On Vinyl shiny side down onto your mat. Follow the instructions by clicking and dragging.
- Weed the excess vinyl and center the pillow cover design once the design has been sliced.
- Use the Easypress Settings Chart to set the timer and temperature for your material.
- Use the Iron-On Protection Sheet to cover the structure, then top it with the Easypress and press the Cricut button. When it has beeped, remove it. Heat for 10 to 15 seconds on the other side of your pillow cover.
- Enable the iron-on to cool before removing the sheet.

7.5. Cricut Gift Boxes

What is the point of creating crafts if you don't gift them? You may even create your own box designs after you've become more comfortable with the Design Space software – nothing beats training for honing a talent. Let's have a look at how you should get started designing your own gift boxes right now.

Materials

- Scoring wheel
- Cardstock (Glitter or of your choice)
- Glue
- Cricut machine

Instructions

- Launch Cricut Design Space and choose "New Project," then import the SVG file patterns you've searched or downloaded. Alternately, start creating your own box patterns.
- Start with the pillowcase package, which is probably the easiest to create for a novice. Using the upper formatting panel in Design Space, resize the patterns to suit the box's expected size. If you're producing more than one box, make sure to click "Ungroup" to distinguish the prototypes that need to be cut and assembled separately. Before submitting the design to cutting, make sure to adjust the Line form to "Score" for any sections of the model that should be folded. After you've finished scoring the lines which have to be folded, pick the whole pattern and click on "Attach," then finish sizing, if necessary, before clicking "Make it."
- When deciding on cutting settings under "Make it," use cardstock as your chosen material. You should start

cutting after you've arranged the material and the cutting pad.

- Assemble the box(es) you'll be using. You won't need to use adhesive to hold the pieces of the box intact if you use light materials like paper or standard cardstock. If you're using glitter cardstock or similar materials, though, you'll need to glue all of the pieces of the package together except the portion that's meant to seal it.
- Begin putting together your package, gluing the pieces that need to be sealed while you move. To help it go smoother and more efficiently, use tacky glue or a glue gun. And your box is all set!

7.6. Personalized Christmas Ornaments

Merry Christmas yall
All is Bright

Materials

- Heat-Resistant Tape
- Cardstock (white)
- Sublimation Ornaments in Blank Form
- Butcher paper
- Mat and EasyPress 2
- Explore Air 2 Machine or Cricut Maker
- Buffalo Check Cricut Infusible Ink Transfer Sheet
- Cloth without any lint

Instructions

- Create your own personalized holiday ornaments by starting a new design in Cricut Design Space.
- For the front and back of each ornament, place two 2.81'' circles. Using the slice feature to generate negative space photographs of the designs within the circle after adding your favorite holiday photos and custom text to the circle.
- Cut your designs with your Cricut machine (ensure to mirror your picture before cutting!) and weed the unwanted Infusible Ink with your fingertips or tweezers.
- Remove any dust, dirt, or smudges from the ornament's surface with a lint-free fabric.
- Apply Infusible Ink on both sections of the blank ornament and cover with heat-resistant tape.

- Preheat the EasyPress 2 to 400°F and set the timer for 240 seconds. Cover with another layer of butcher paper after placing the ornaments on top of the butcher paper.
- Place the EasyPress 2 on top of the decorations for 240 seconds; just don't press down! Place the EasyPress 2 back on its base after the loop is over, then carefully peel the top layer of butcher paper.

7.7 Christmas Tea Towels

Christmas tea towels are a simple and quick way to get started with the Cricut cutting unit. Simply use heat transfer vinyl to provide almost limitless design options.

Materials

- Tea towel with a deer silhouette
- Tea towel "Merry and Bright."
- flour sack towels (white)
- Cut files and iron-on for Christmas tea towels.
- Tool for weeding
- press cloth or parchment paper.
- Iron or EasyPress
- Cricut Explore Air 2 or Cricut Maker

Instructions

- In Design Space, open the Christmas tea towel cut file(s).
- Adjust the sizes and colors to your liking. Don't neglect to mirror the text while cutting the iron-on vinyl for your Christmas tea towels.
- Choose the materials. The cutting material on the Cricut Maker is selected directly in Design Space; many of the most popular cutting material choices may appear.
- With the weeder unit, remove any negative space from the designs.
- Place the patterns on the towel with the liners and see where you like them.

- Set the EasyPress's temperature and timer according to the instructions for the material you're ironing on and the material you're ironing on to. Preheat the tea towel by ironing it to prevent any wrinkles. Cover the pattern with the press cloth or parchment paper and press down tightly for the period shown on the map. To begin the timer, press the right-hand Cricut button. Enable the liners to cool down for a moment after the timer goes off before trying to peel them off. Replace the filler and click for another 5–10 seconds if some aspect of the pattern starts to pull up.

Chapter 8: Tips And Trick

Using a Cricut is a thrilling experience. For a novice, it may even be intimidating and daunting. These 28 Cricut Tricks and Secrets can save your sanity and help you remain more organized along the way, whether you're a newcomer or a professional Cricut crafter.

8.1 Cricut Tricks and Secrets

1. Peel the mat instead of material

While it can sound natural to peel the material (vinyl, cardstock, etc.) away from the surface, it is simply preferable to softly curl and peel the mat away from the stuff. This helps to save the art supplies from being so distorted.

2. For vinyl storage, use IKEA plastic bags.

IKEA plastic bag storage holders are another favorite Cricut hacks that have gained some attention in recent years. They're great for keeping vinyl rolls. You can even get some on the internet!

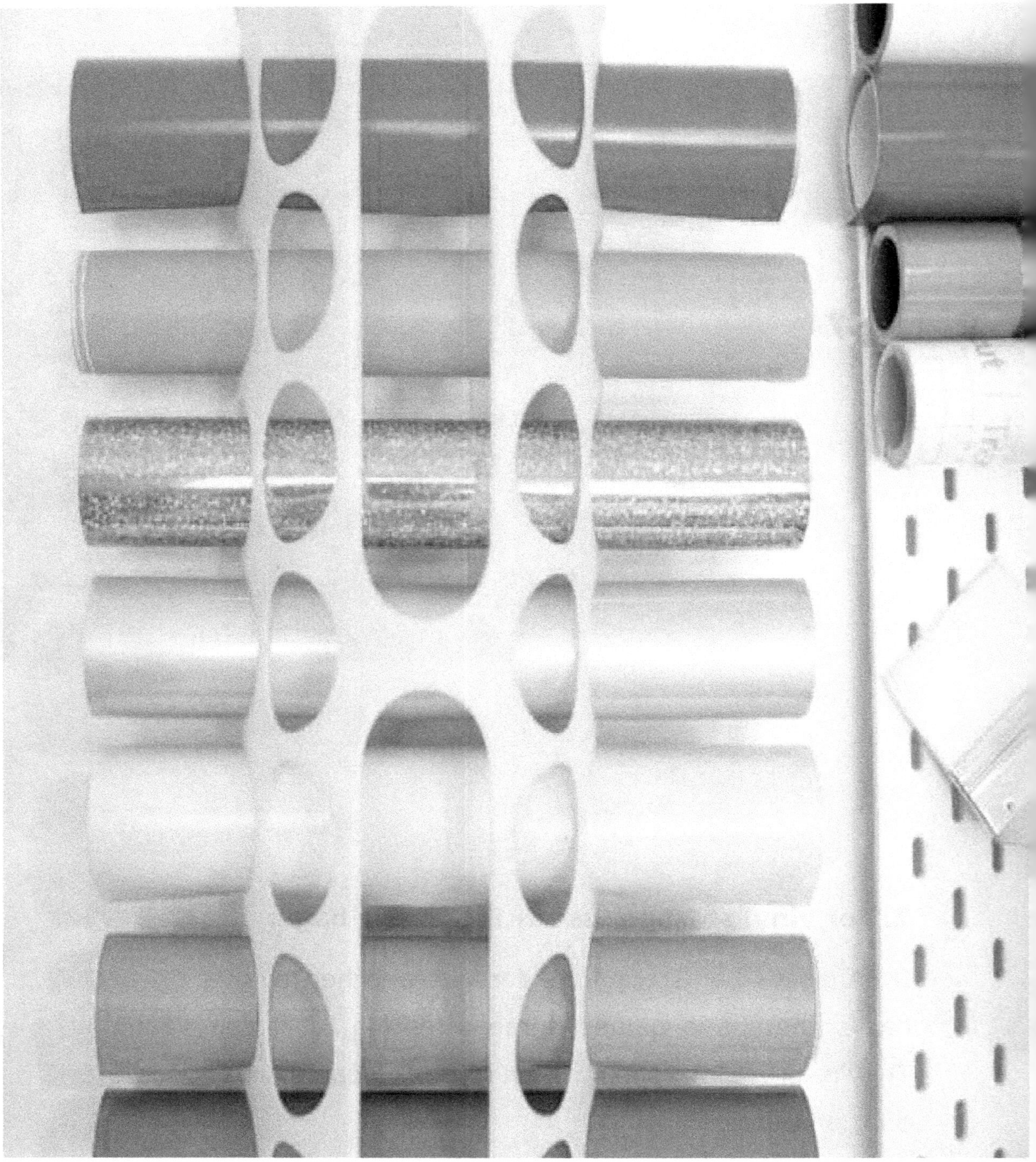

3. Tin foil should be used to sharpen the razor.

Sharpening the fine-point blade with tin foil will quickly prolong its life! In reality, using tin foil will extend the blade's life by three times! Remove the blade from the clamp and pass the edge 10-12 times through the tin foil with the blade to sharpen it.

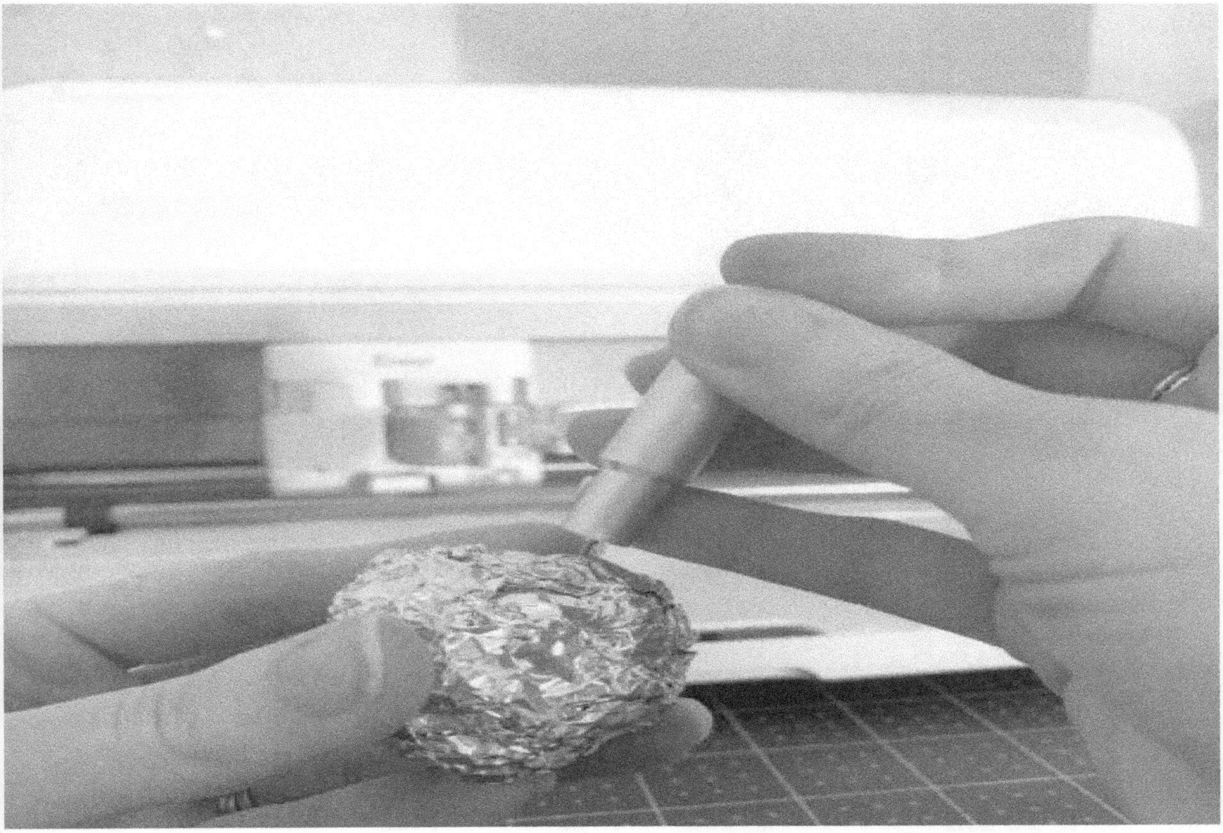

4. keep your knives in the Cricut.

This could seem self-evident, but as a novice Cricut user, you may have no idea that the interior of your system could store the blades and small tools in a dust-free, secure manner.

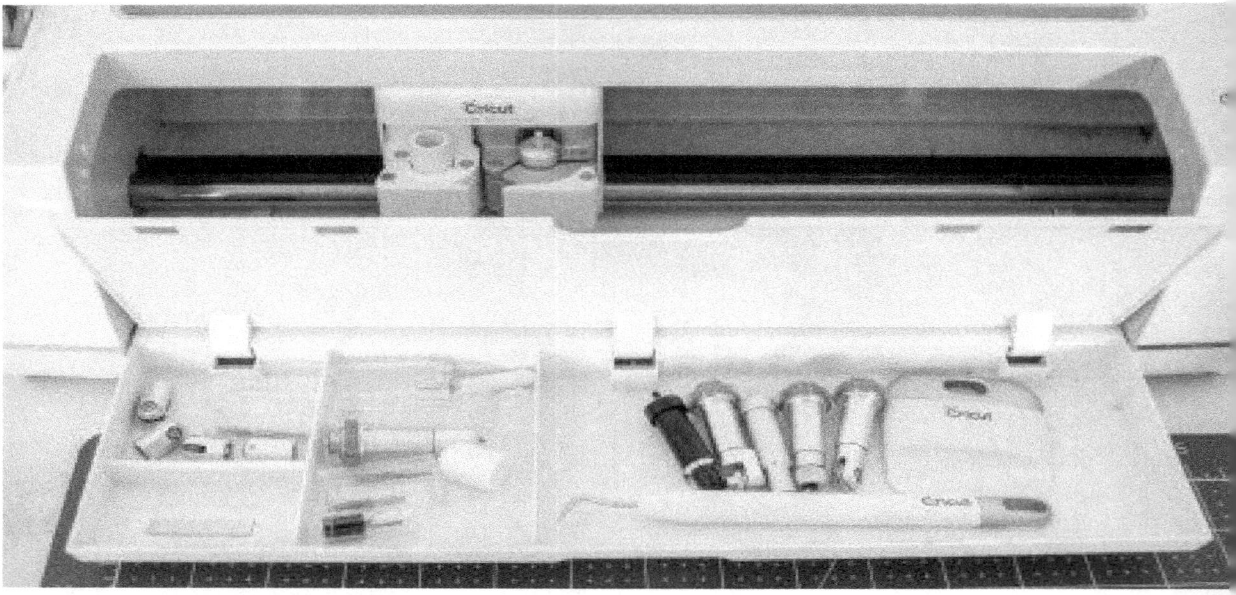

5. Pick up little fragments from your pad or pattern with a lint roller (Works for glitter too)

You should quickly catch the excess little bits on a lint roller if you have an elaborate pattern cut out on paper or vinyl to save time!

It's still great for picking up stray glitter on your desk.

6. In spite of using Cricut pens for your laptop, use pen adapters.

The ability to have your Cricut machine compose for you is a fantastic function. You'll actually wish you could use pens rather than Cricut pens at some stage.

The good news is that if you have an Explore 2 or later, you can buy pen adapters that will enable you to use almost any brand of a pen! Sharpies, brush pens, and more are all available!

How to Use ALL these Pens with Your Cricut!
1. Sharpie Fine Point
2. Sharpie Ultra Fine Point
3. Sharpie Pen Art Pen
4. Pilot Precise
5. Bic Marking
6. Bic Cristal
7. Sakura Gelly Roll
8. Amaza Gel Pens
9. Sharpie Oil-Based Paint
10. Uni-ball Signo UM-153
11. Crayola Fine Line Marker
12. Crayola Super Tip
13. Crayola Detailing Gel Pen
14. Tombow Duel Brush Pens

7. For vinyl remnants, use a nail polish tray.

One of most favorite Cricut hacks is this one! When weeding, get a cheap nail polish holder to catch tiny vinyl bits.

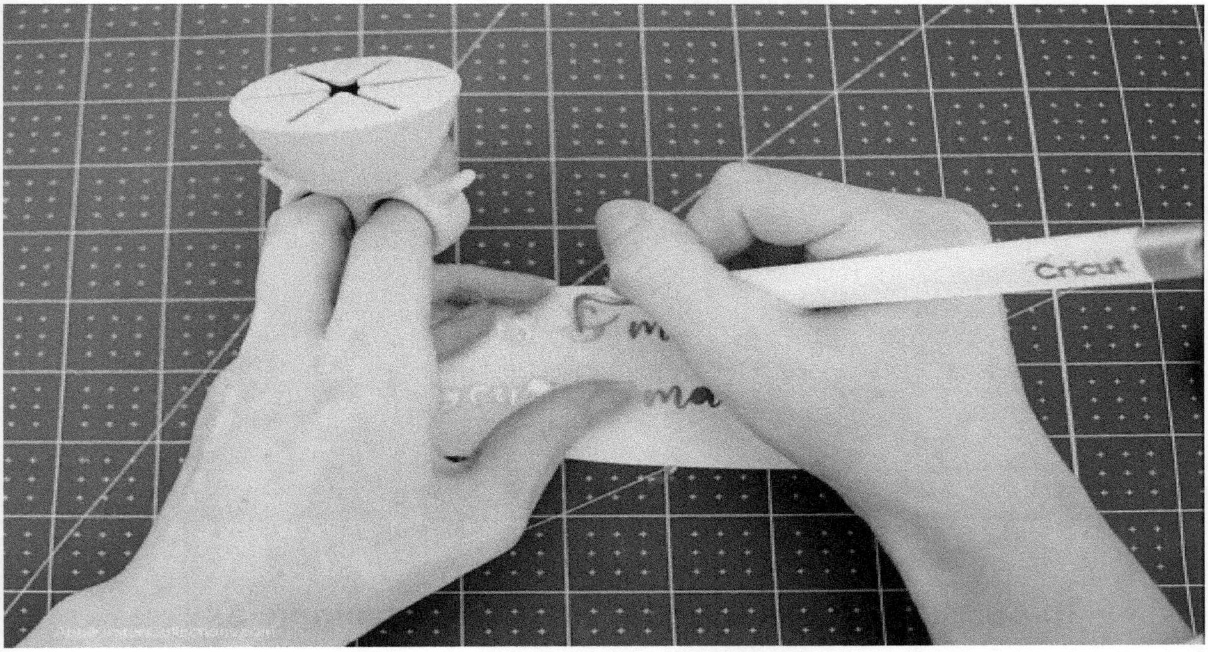

8. Inkscape is a free program that allows you to create your own SVG cut files.

SVG files for Design Space can be found for free or purchased by Cricut Access. So what if you had your own?

After all, there are occasions when there is a need to introduce a specific vision to life or customize an object. Inkscape is a free, open-source software for creating SVG files from nothing or converting images to layered SVG files.

9. Converting a picture to an SVG is as simple as clicking a button

If you aren't ready to learn how to build your own SVG files, use the one-click picture to SVG converter instead.

10. Use a pegboard to keep all of your Cricut materials organized

Pegboards are vital for keeping supplies ordered, and you can save money by using unused wall space! These can be used at Amazon or on IKEA. Plus, Cricut hacks like this really help to make your craft room look nice.

11. Baby wipes may be used to clean your mat. Resticky the mat with Easy Tack

Cleaning the dirt off of recycled Cricut mats with baby wipes will give them a new lease on existence. You may even re-sticky every mat for another 5-10 uses by spraying it with a few coats of Easy Tack.

12. To hold vinyl rolls tight, use slap bracelets.

If you have a lot of vinyl, then keep the rolls in a variety of places. Slap bracelets are an inexpensive way to keep vinyl rolls intact.

13. Sort the vinyl into wood bins by type.

It's important to keep track of your vinyl styles (iron-on, textured, adhesive, etc.). Bins may be a convenient way to organize items by category and mark each bin for easy identification.

14. Trim vinyl with a smooth edge to prevent rough corners.

If you're not patient, vinyl is one of the materials that can easily be thrown away. Trimming the vinyl before cutting can help hold the edges straight and reduce waste.

15. Discover fantastic SVG freebies

Free SVG files for Design Space can be listed on Pinterest searches, among other sites. There is a huge Freebie Vault at Abbi Kirsten Collections of over 150 free SVG and printable models!

16. For tougher fabrics, use painter's tape

Painters tape will be your best buddy if your things are rolling around on your mat. It's particularly relevant when working with wood and chipboard.

17. When adding vinyl to angled surfaces, cut slits in the transfer tape.

On a curved wall, how can you get the vinyl to be smooth?

Aside from practice, one technique is to make slits along the edges of the transfer tape. This gives the tape some wiggle room when you position the pattern.

18. Use cheat sheets to help you remember what each feature does.

Understanding Cricut terminology and the features in Design Space may be difficult to remember; a glossary cheat sheet may be very useful. You can also get it online.

19. Use a magazine holder to store vinyl remnants.

Don't throw out the odd and ends of vinyl! Small cuts can also be made for them. To see what you have to deal from, keep your scraps in a plain magazine holder.

20. Make use of a printable environment guide

Trying to recall any of those content settings or custom settings, much as Design Space features is almost difficult! There is a free guide on the subject that you can find inside the Freebie Vault!

21. On wood, use iron-on vinyl (HTV).

Well, indeed! Iron-on vinyl should be used on wood! To make it easier, Cricut has heat guidance. The look of heat transfer vinyl to that of adhesive vinyl is preferred mostly.

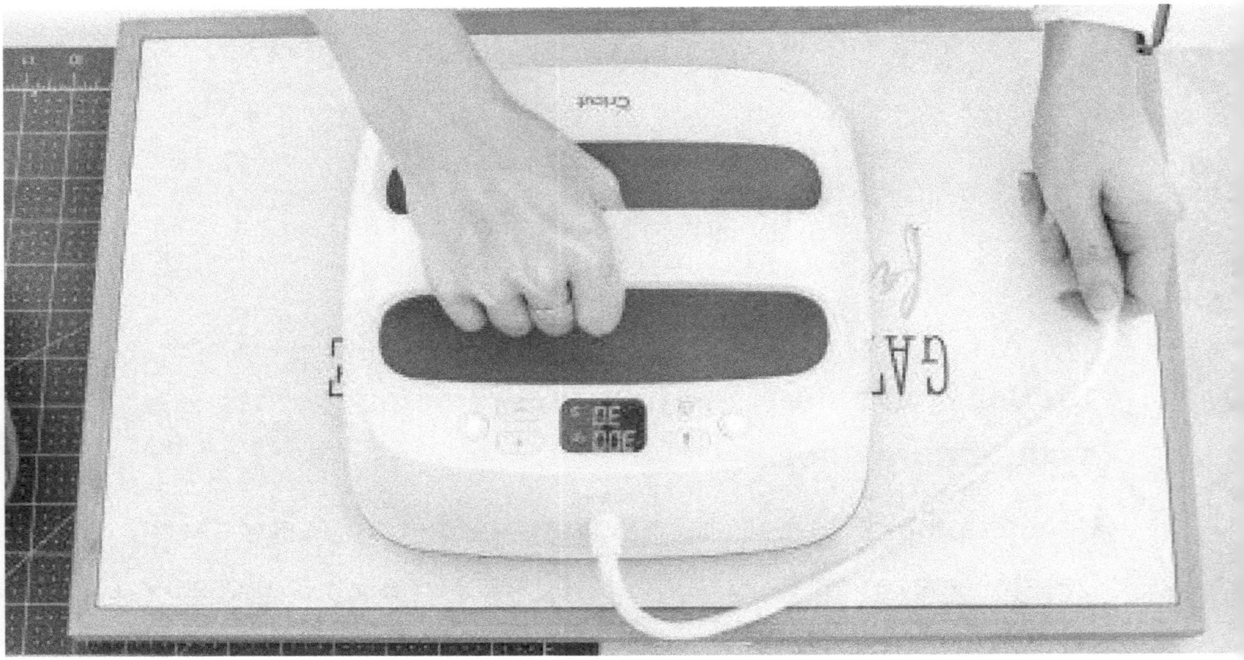

22. Use the Cricut Easy Mini-Press to apply iron-on vinyl to tumblers.

In 2019, Cricut launched the Easypress Micro, a miniature variant of the Easypress. This little gadget is so adorable and useful that it also allows you to iron on vinyl to your tumblers!

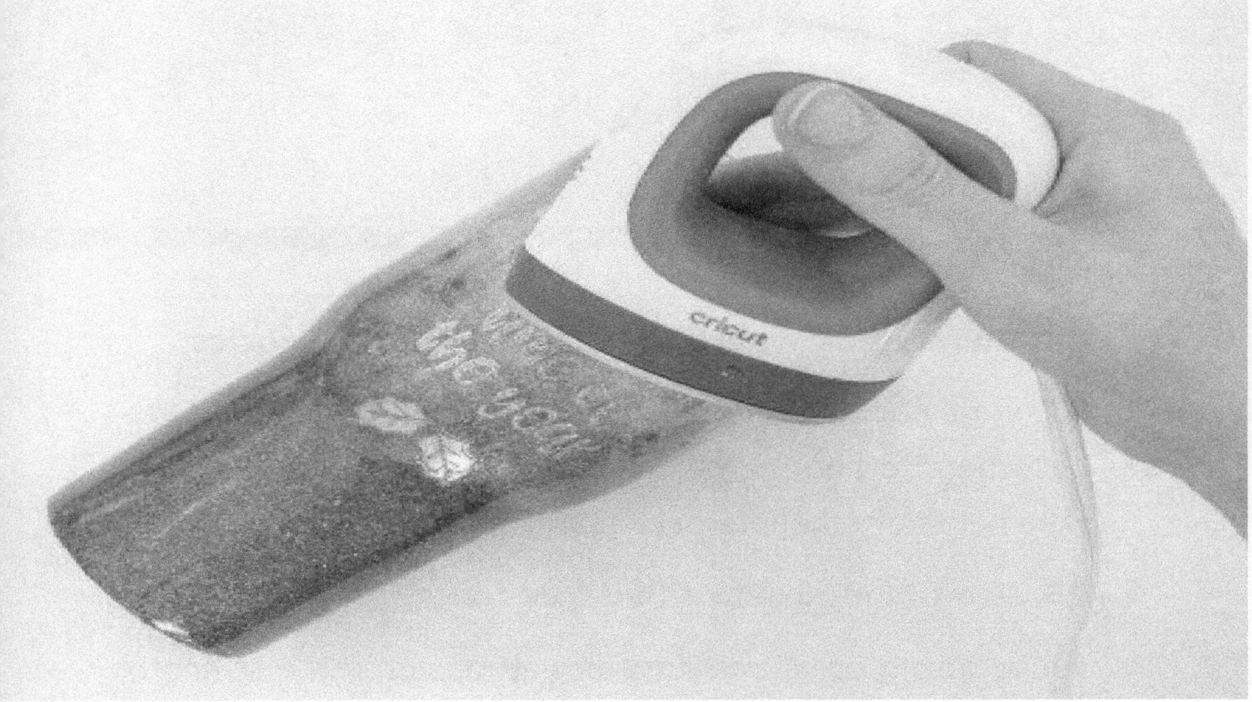

23. Freebies can be found in the Cricut Design Room.

Did you realize that every week, Cricut releases a new package of freebies that anybody can use, even if they don't have Cricut Access?! Freebies can be found under Images > Filter > Freebies!

24. Understand where to look for the right fabrics

It can take a long time and a lot of trial and error to figure out where to find the best-priced Cricut products. You can take help from the internet regarding this.

25. Use the internet to find free fonts.

You're losing out if you haven't yet mastered the strength of downloading free fonts for your Cricut. Check out the internet for the top 60 free and paid fonts, as well as exclusive Christmas font posts!

26. Import specialty projects to build a room using character maps

It's one thing to download fonts, but it's quite another to learn how to make a word appear like a million bucks! It took me a while to figure out that you can navigate those unique scrolly letters using your computer's "character charts" or "glyphs."

1. Go to your PC's "search" function and look for "character map" or "character viewer" on the Mac.

2. Pick your preferred font from the drop-down menu.

3. Scroll down before you reach the letter you're looking for.

4. Pick it with a click, then copy it.

5. In Design Space, paste the font character into the text box.

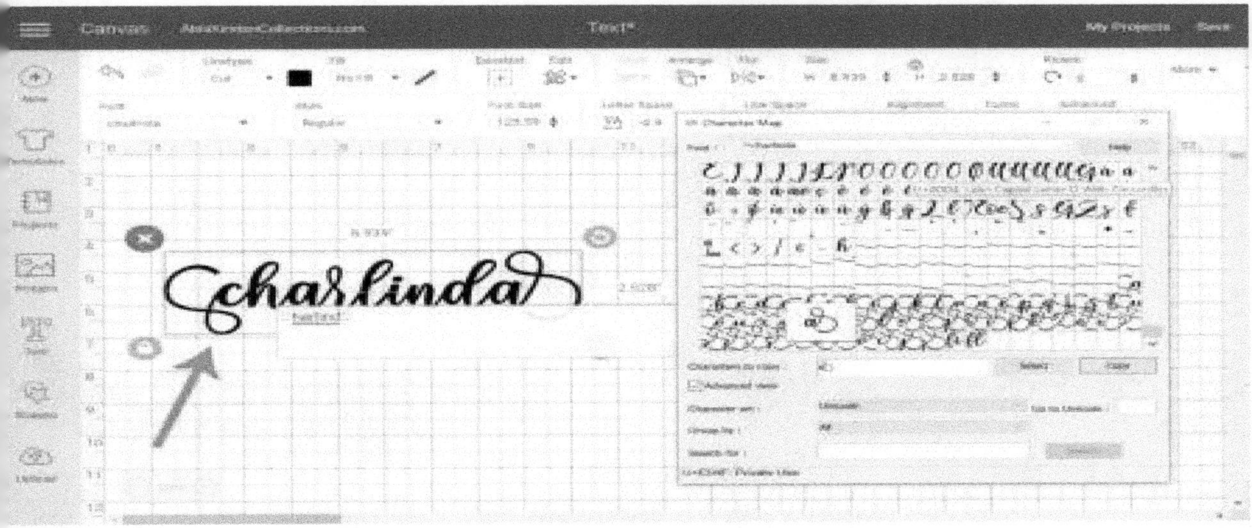

27. Maintain a list of your favorite vinyl records.

There is so much vinyl that it's difficult to keep track of them all! There are several styles, textures, and labels of vinyl to keep track of. To keep track, keep pieces of vinyl on a metal ring labeled with the brand and form of vinyl so you can still locate your favorite vinyl!

28. Keep supplies and machines in storage carts.

It's important to keep the supplies and machinery secure. A storage rolling cart is one of the favorite ways to do this! Check out your nearest Michaels shop!

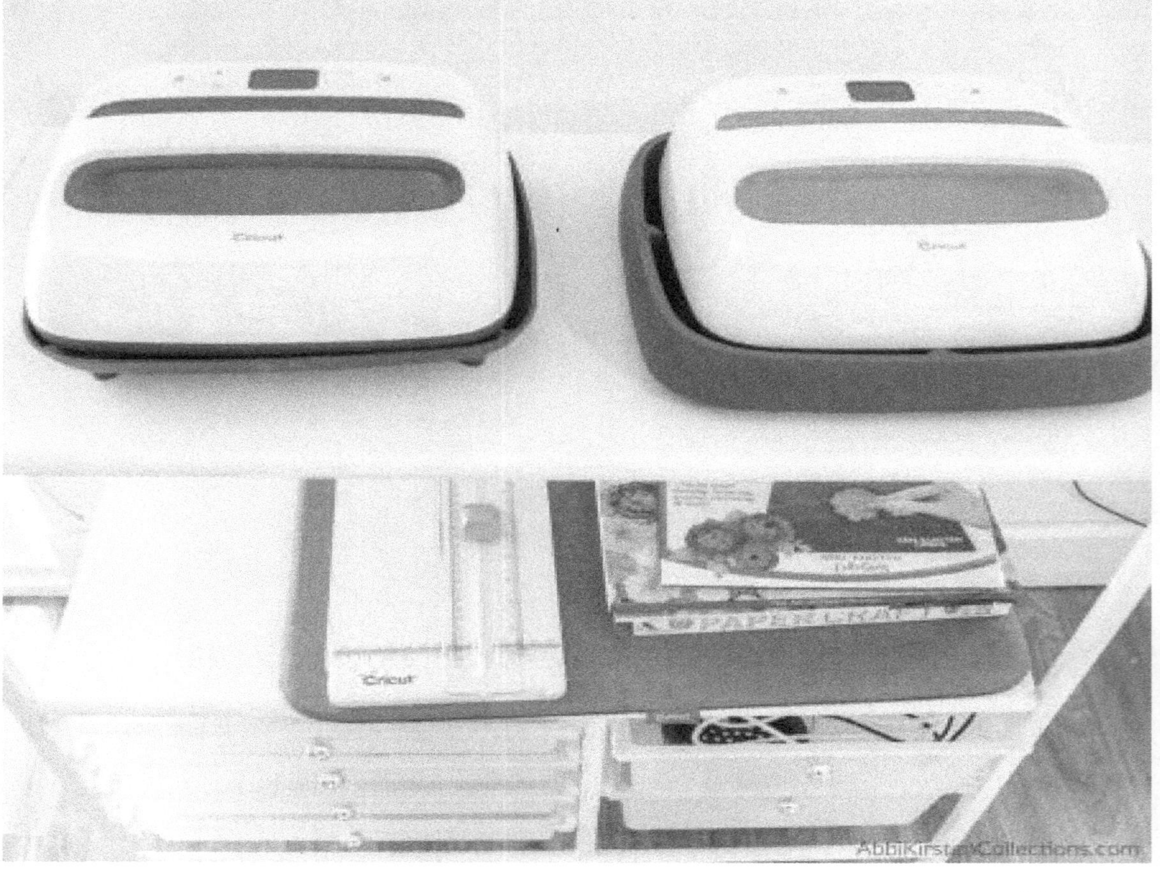

8.2 Mat Maintenance and Longevity

Since the mats are costly, you will want to retain them in service for a long time. The best way to extend the existence of a mat is to treat it carefully and properly. Here are some tips about how to take control of these mats:

- After each use, replace the transparent cover/film on the sheet. Which will keep the mat clean and free of dirt and dust.
- Use a lint roller to remove any substance debris from the mat surface during each use.
- Use non-alcoholic wipes to clean the mat.

• Wash the mats with soapy water, except for the silk mat. The cotton mat is unlike any other mat in that it cannot be washed with water.

• Using a scraper, clean any object debris from the mat surface except the cloth mat.

8.3 Cricut Maker Specialty Equipment

Aside from the blades, there are other specialized instruments for purposes other than cutting.

Markers and pens

There is a space for markers and pens next to the blade housing. If you want to design greeting cards and want to use elegant fonts, this is the place to go. The Cricut is compatible with a wide range of pens and markers. Markers and pens must be purchased separately.

Scoring Wheel

This is a one-of-a-kind feature. This scoring wheel is your buddy if you don't need to cut a pattern but only need to fold a piece of material. This feature can be used for a variety of things, like creating personalized crates and making a Greeting card.

Single and double scoring tips are the two forms of scoring tips available. Depending on the project, you will use the same housing with all styles of tips.

Fast Swap Housing and Helpful Tips

This is sole housing that can be used for a variety of feature tips. The tips that can be used colloquially with this housing are explained in the following section.

Foil Transfer Tip

This is one of the most recent Cricut Maker functions. This is used to embellish and bling up the finished products. It's designed to be used with foil covers.

Deboss tip

This tip is similar to the engraving tip, but it is designed for finer, lighter materials. Foil, dense card paper, and basswood may all be decorated with it.

Engrave tip

This tip may be used to engrave texts or monograms on a variety of items. Plastic mats, leather and metal sheets are the best materials for this. With this tip, you will make the projects more special.

Perforation Tip

Tear-off materials are often used for a project. The perforation tip is used for this reason. This tip works well for lightweight fabrics.

Wavy tip

This tip can come in handy when creating greeting cards. This results in wavy edges, which provide a decorative touch. It may be used to embellish card corners, as well as iron-on vinyl and other textured sheets.

Conclusion

Surely, after reading this book, you've come to the conclusion that the Cricut Machine is the perfect tool for creative people. This die-cut machine offers a wide range of options for anyone. The Cricut Machine takes your ideas and transforms them into truth. The device's best features are its dependability and accuracy. A crafter's ultimate goal is perfection, which is just what the Cricut delivers.

Cricut's Design Space program is another important feature. It is the software that allows you to monitor and create on the computer. The biggest feature about it is that it has a really user-friendly GUI. In only a few clicks, you'll be able to continue with your designs and DIYs. This app can be downloaded and used offline on your machine or mobile. You may either start from scratch in the Design Space or choose from a variety of pre-made designs in the software.

So, if you're a creative person who enjoys creating lovely things for yourself, your family, friends, or even a company, the Cricut Machine is the machine for you.

Cricut Project

A Step By Step guide to Learn How To Master Your Cutting Machine, Design Space, Accessories & Tools With Tips & Tricks to Create The Projects Of Your Dreams

By

Mia Gomez

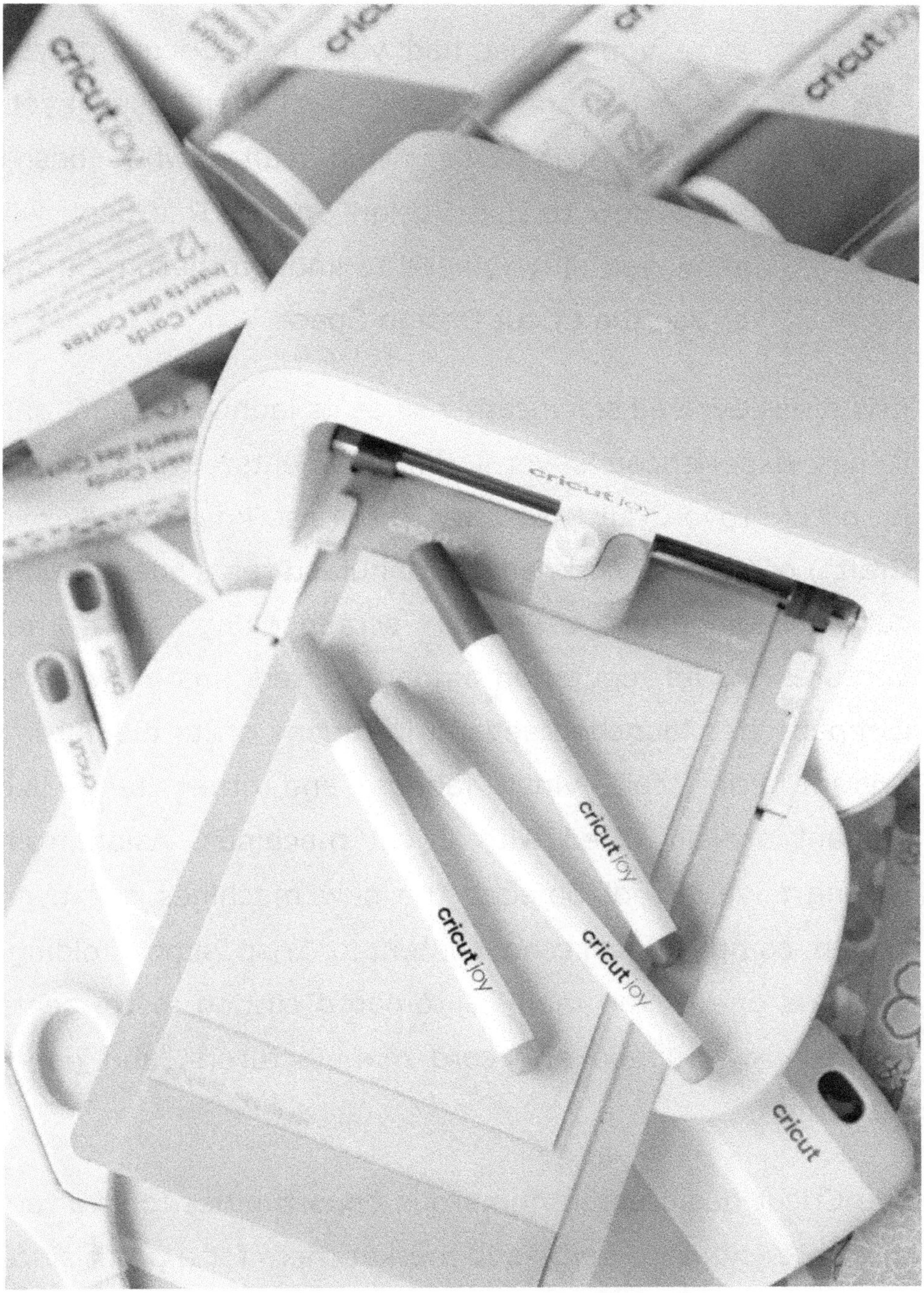
cricut joy
cricut joy
cricut joy
cricut joy
cricut

Introduction

Maybe you've just had your first Cricut; maybe you've had one for a while but haven't used it yet; maybe you're a seasoned crafter who doesn't know how to use Design Space. This book will show you all you need to know to become a pro to use the Cricut Design Space.

Cricut has evolved significantly since its launch in 2006, and it has experienced several improvements. Cricut is the brand of Provo Craft & Novelty, Inc. (also known as "Provo Craft") of Spanish Fork, which manufactures a line of home cutting equipment used for scrapbooking and other ventures. As its reputation among crafters has grown, the company has launched several iterations of its die-cutting system. Print, felt, vinyl, fabrics, and other items like fondant are all sliced with Cricut machines. Aside from cutting a variety of objects, the new machines can even sketch, compose, and score content for crisp, simple folding. Cricut is one of the many automated cutting instruments utilized by scrapbookers, card manufacturers, and paper craftsmen.

The Cricut has created numerous opportunities for crafters to create exquisite items and market them for a profit since its creation.

Some Cricut operators have perfected the device to the point that they can render vinyl letters that appear to be drawn on wood. You won't be able to locate a place to pick either one of the vinyl characters with the human eye because the vinyl blends too well. That's how true it will appear. In addition, the majority of types of vinyl are weather-resistant. That allows designers to create a wide range of fantastic items for both the inside and outside of your home.

Cricut has come a long way from the days of die-cutting for scrapbooking, and while scrapbooking is still common, you won't see too many sheets of stickers in supermarkets and the scrapbooking area of certain stores has shrunk as Cricut has evolved into so many more than a scrapbooking companion.

Best of all, several Cricut models support Bluetooth, making it simple to connect with other users.

One of the best things about a Cricut system is how little room it takes up. It's almost the same size as a home printer, but you'll need a lot of room for your equipment and supplies. Is it correct to claim that you're trying to figure out what there is to know about Cricut Design Space and don't know where to start?

Until cutting the projects, much of the magic happens on the outside of Cricut's framework space. Here, one can organize, modify, and save their embodiments. You can not only use and transfer your textual patterns and pictures in this region, but you can also use top-quality Cricut images and text styles via individual purchases, such as Cricut Access and Cartridges.

The Cricut shaper device is one of the most common Cricut pieces. Any dedicated specialty laborer may make various shapes and plans by inserting its cartridge into the shaper. Provided its exceptional preparation guide, many people put aside a large sum of money for this device. Cricut didn't only inspire creativity by craftsmanship; it also rendered scrapbooking fun and accessible to all. Indeed, even those of limited abilities will now be capable of creating their pieces of art.

Chapter 1: What is a Cricut Machine?

A Cricut is a cutting device – that's the simple answer – that can cut and create excellent artworks out of materials you had no idea existed. Think of it like a printer: you create a picture or a painting on your screen and submit it to the system. Rather than printing your template, the Cricut machine cuts it out of whatever stuff you choose!

1.1. Brief history of Cricut

A Cricut device resembles a printer, but rather than printing ink; it uses tools to carve shapes into various fabrics. The very first Cricut was easy enough to use without the use of a monitor. To signify the prints to remove, it used clear cartridges placed into a tray.

Cricut technology is still improving, but the first versions were still designed to operate without the use of a computer. All of that changed in 2014, when Cricut Explore, the first idea that needed a computer, was revealed. Rather than focusing exclusively on cartridges, this system makes use of Cricut Design Space, an online program that serves as both a help program and a basic design tool.

Since Cricut is now compatible with the computing machine, it is compatible with third-party applications as well as a broad range of online sources and models. For artists, the Cricut has become an imperative tool. Cricut's technology has progressed to the point that devices will now attach wirelessly to your tablet or mobile and do more than just repair it. It also contains equipment like labeling wheels, calligraphy pencil carriers, and blades for tougher fabrics, in addition to rotary blades.

1.2. Cricut unique features

Some unique features of Cricut cutting equipment's are listed below:

- Cuts up to 2x quicker.
- Cuts more than 100 different materials.
- Create totally private.
- Easy to learn and use.
- Print and cut.
- Design anytime you are motivated.
- Thousands of patterns to choose from

1.3. How do Cricut Machines work?

A Cricut machine cuts a pattern out of a piece of paper (or other material) with a thin, movable cutter. To begin, use Cricut's design software or application to build a design. Then, using Bluetooth or USB, you submit the specification to the Cricut unit. The template is fed into the Cricut system, which then cuts it out with a thin, precise cutter.

Here's how to use a Cricut in basic words.

- Place the sticky cutting mat on top of the cutting stuff. (While the Cricut produces the cuts, the cutting pad keeps the material in place.) Place the mat in the unit and turn it on.
- Open Cricut Design Space and choose a design. Send the pattern to your Cutting machine after selecting your materials settings.
- To begin cutting, push the button on your unit.
- Remove the mat from the device and the material attached until the machine has finished cutting.

1.4. What would a Cricut Machine do for me?

The following is a selection of the most common items it will produce:

- Create scrapbooking letters, sentences, and forms by designing and cutting them out.
- Create scrapbooking and labeling terms and quotations.
- Create stickers for your notebook, calendar, or anything else you'd like.
- Use beautiful fonts to address envelopes.

- Make personalized invitations for birthdays, anniversaries, and other special events, such as teacher appreciation presents on Teacher's Day.
- Create your own Erin Condren planner stickers.
- Build and design personalized t-shirts and sweatshirts.
- Make decorations for a celebration or a picnic.
- Design and make customized infant onesies.
- Make perfect drip cakes by cutting out handmade cake toppers.
- Make decals for the walls.
- Create window decals and cut them off.
- Create your own earring.
- Create or cut out interior painting stencils.
- Make a framed quotation art piece.
- Make a drawn or carved wooden sign.
- Create a monogram or matching pillows.
- Create a name badge for your pet.
- Create an ineffable leather bracelet.
- Create your own Christmas Decorations.
- Transform socks into amusing presents by personalizing them.
- Make wine cups, mugs, and tumblers decorations.
- Create decals for whatever you choose to personalize.
- Create a unique plate by decorating regular plates.

- Make personalized pantry, wardrobe, and organizational stickers.
- Make buntings and banners out of paper.
- Create personalized vinyl car stickers and cut them out.

...as well as several other do-it-yourself or crafty projects.

1.5. Types of Cricut Machines

Cricut devices come in a variety of shapes and sizes. Cricut machines are divided into four categories, each of which is used to cut out different designs. Some types of Cricut, including Cricut Expression, Cricut Expression 2, and Cricut Explore, are legacy machines. The Cricut Cuttlebug was widely used for die-cutting and embossing, but it's been discontinued as of spring 2019.

1.5.1 Cricut Maker

The Cricut Maker is the most up-to-date and efficient cutting machine available. It can cut over 300 different fabrics, including wood, cloth, felt, silk, acrylic, and plastic. It also handles mats ranging 12 *12 inches or 12 * 24 inches. The Cricut Maker also has a modern Adaptive Tool System, which gives it more flexibility and expandability. You can now use engraving, grading, debossing, and perforating results (and plenty of other things) on your artistic creations using a variety of modern materials.

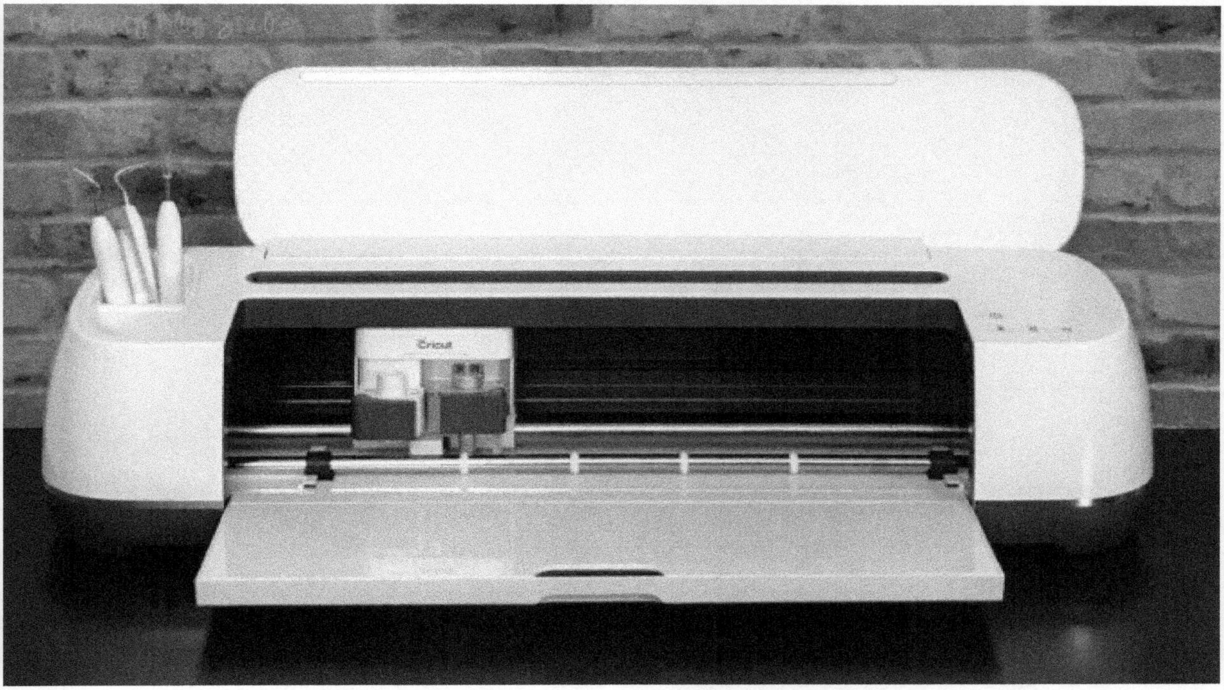

Figure 1.1: The Cricut Maker

The Knife Blade, for example, can cut through surfaces (Chipboard, basswood, tooled leather) as thick as 2.4 mm thick. Cutting fabrics is much easier with the supplied Rotary Blade.

1.5.2 Cricut Explore 1

The Cricut Explore 1, the first of its kind, was truly revolutionary. This affordable machine allows both trainees and experts to do precision cutting. It's ideal for a wide range of DIY projects and designs.

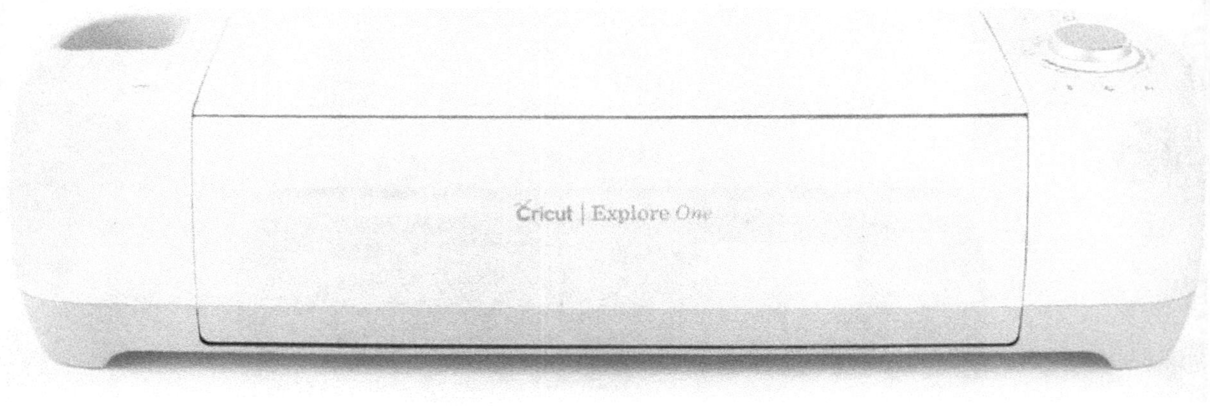

Figure 1.2: Cricut Explore One

You may use the Explore One to create your own fonts and SVGs or select from the Cricut Image Library's tens of thousands of graphic files. This machine was easy to operate and worked well with home computers. It had storage containers for extra knives, pens, and other products, as well as the ability to use it with a Bluetooth adaptor.

1.5.3 Cricut Explore Air

The Explore Air is a wireless device that can cut a wide range of objects, from paper to cloth and anything in between. It's compatible with the latest Circuit Design Space app. The Cricut Explore Air is a level drop from the Air 2, but it has two features that the Explore 1 does not: it is Bluetooth-enabled, so you don't have to plug it in, and it has a tool holder to compose, rate, and cut all at once.

Figure 1.3: Cricut Explore Air

The number of products that can be sliced with the Air has grown to include over 60 different options. Though there is always a spot for a Cricut Cartridge to be inserted, the model files are connected to your account, so you can get rid of the cartridge.

1.5.4 Cricut Explore Air 2

The Cricut Explore Air Two is a wireless cutting system that is quicker and saves time. When compared to its predecessors, this system is near twice as quick. There are over a hundred different materials that can be used.

Figure 1.4: Cricut Explore Air 2

It has a large library of photographs and previously prepared designs to pick from, as well as Smart Set materials settings that are quickly changed, and CutSmart technology that cuts precisely depending on the chosen material.

1.6. Cricut tools

Cricut provides a few cheap hand tools to help you create much more with your Cricut. Here are a few of top options for your machine to consider:

- **Wavy tool**: This tool aids in the development of waves in your design.
- **Bright pad**: This tool aids in the visibility of the lines that ought to be cut. If you're doing more than one cut, this will come in handy because it will aid in tracing and pattern adaptation.
- **Scraping tool**: This keeps the material from sliding about when removing some little parts from the design.
- **Paper trimmer**: This is useful for clear cuts since it eliminates the need for a ruler or scissors. It's needed while dealing with vinyl.
- **Perforation tool**: Perforated marks in your design are made easier with this tool.

- **Tweezers**: These are useful for removing small bits of vinyl from the center without scratching or dragging the corners.
- **Easy press Tool**: This is great for iron-on vinyl, which doesn't need to be ironed. It still keeps the vinyl in better shape, even though you wear it a lot, and reduces the need for temperature and time guesswork. While it is a little expensive, there are novice choices available.
- **Weeding tool**: When dealing with vinyl, this is one of the safest methods to have since it aids in the removal of vinyl from the backing sheets.
- **Brayer**: Whether you're using a cloth or bigger bits of vinyl, it is one of the better tools for keeping the material stable on your mat and preventing harm to the mat.
- **Spatula**: This is a perfect one because it allows you to remove the pattern from the backing without damaging the paper and keeps it clean.
- **Scissors**: Cricut scissors are constructed of stainless steel and have micro-tip blades, making them ideal for fine work.
- **Backup mats**: This should go without saying, but if you're working on a bigger project, the mats will lose their stickiness with time. This would save you from needing to stop working on your project to take up anything else.

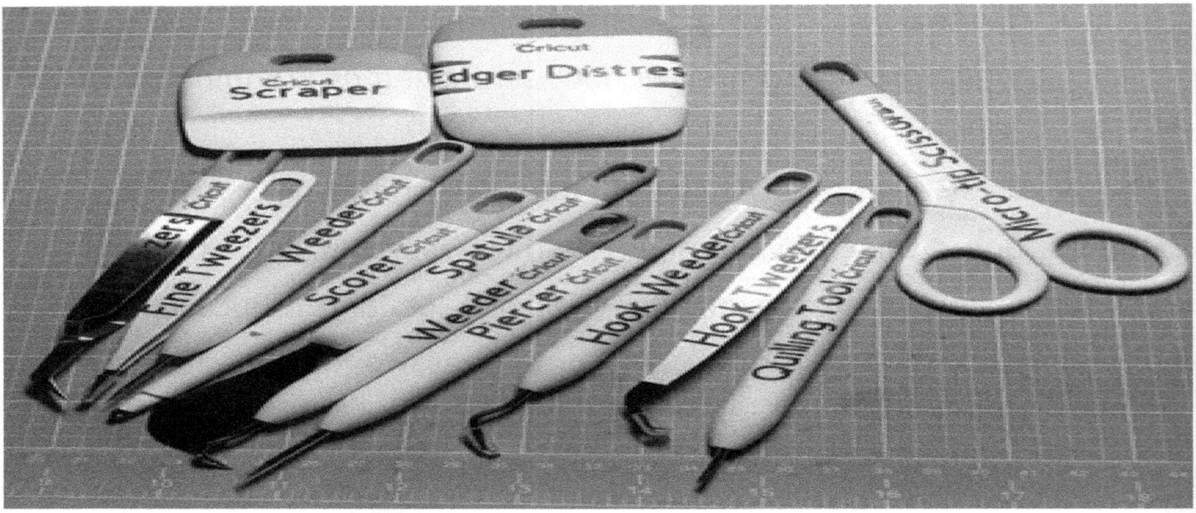

Figure 1.5: Cricut Essential tools

These tools are important, and you'll want to have the toolset to get the initial few on the list since it's much cheaper. However, if you plan on using your device often, it's strongly recommended that you invest a little extra money on equipment to go with it.

1.7 What materials can be cut with a Cricut Machine?

Cricut can cut so many distinct materials that the creativity is the only limit. These incredible devices can do everything from fragile notebook paper to hard leathers. Most materials can be cut on all Cricut machines. All the cutting and application instructions for the following materials have been provided by the Cricut at their website Help Centre.

1.7.1 Paper, Cardstock, Art Board, Insert Cards

- Pearl Paper
- Glitter Cardstock
- Corrugated Cardboard Collection
- Washi Sheets
- Printable Clear Sticker Paper
- Cricut Kraft Board
- Cricut Foil Paper
- Foil Poster Board
- Deluxe Paper, Adhesive Backed
- Printable Sticker Paper
- Poster Board
- Deluxe Paper
- Cricut Joy Smart Label Writable Paper

1.7.2 Iron-On

- Foil Iron-On
- Glitter Mesh Iron-On
- Glitter Iron-On
- Holographic Iron-On
- Express Iron-On
- Cricut Joy Smart Iron-On
- Everyday Iron-On
- Express Iron-On
- Holographic Sparkle Iron-On
- Mosaic Iron-On
- Patterned Iron-On
- Sport Flex Iron-On
- Cricut Joy Smart Iron-On
- Everyday Iron-On Mesh

1.7.3 Vinyl

- Adhesive Foil, Matte
- Cricut Joy Smart Vinyl
- Dry Erase Vinyl
- Glitter Vinyl
- Premium Vinyl - Removable
- Holographic Vinyl
- Premium Glossy Outdoor Vinyl
- Premium Vinyl Shimmer - Permanent
- Stencil Vinyl
- Chalkboard Vinyl

- Printable Vinyl
- Adhesive Foil
- Premium Vinyl - Permanent
- Cricut Joy Smart Label Writable Vinyl

1.7.4 Felt, Foam & Metal

- Foil Acetate
- Craft Foam
- Cricut Aluminum Sheets
- Party Foil
- Deluxe Paper Foil Embossed

1.7.5 Fabric

- Cricut Fusible Cloth
- Printable Fabric
- Cricut Maker Fusible Cloth

1.7.6 Other

- Printable Magnet Sheets
- Window Cling

Chapter 2: Setting up Cricut Machine on Design Space

Its critical to figure out where you'll place your Cricut machine before you start cutting. The device should be located near a desktop or tablet and an energy source, and enough space to run. And if the equipment doesn't need to be connected to a computer, hold it close by to allow loading and unloading to go more smoothly.

It's also a good idea to think of the space around or above the unit. For the mats to travel around as desired, a length of 10 inches in front and rear is optimal. To ensure that the mats lie down, the area in front of the device should be smooth and aligned with the machine. Most materials would not work well if the mats are not flat. Twelve inches above the unit is needed to install tools conveniently.

What is Design Space?

The free design program that is used with each Cricut machine is called Design Space. It is very user-friendly and thus simple to use. It's a cloud-based software service, which ensures you can view all of your project data from any computer with an Internet connection.

No matter what Cricut you have, there are *three crucial steps* to connecting and trying to set up your Cricut.

1. Downloading and installing the Design Space app
2. Connecting the unit to your desktop
3. Connect your machine to your Cricut account.

Since each operative model is distinct, the first two stages appear differently on each unit. However, since you'll be using the same interface, pairing your computer with your Cricut Accounts would be somewhat similar.

2.1. Installing Design space

Design Space software is available for Windows, Mac, iOS, and Android, allowing you to operate on a variety of devices.

The majority of newer Cricut machines have Bluetooth capabilities, making it simple to link to mobile devices. Cricut used to have an "Online" version that required access to the internet. You will access the App offline from your computer or iOS device after you've downloaded it (not android).

Important: To download and log in to this program, you must have access to the internet.

2.1.1 For Windows

The steps to install design space on Windows are as follows.

- Go to https://design.cricut.com via your web browser.
- Choose "download" from the drop-down menu.
- Wait for the file to complete before proceeding.
- Open the file in the tab or in the download folder when it's finished downloading.
- The installation progress is shown in a setup window.
- Enter your Cricut Username and password to log in.
- A Design Space icon appears on the desktop automatically. To pin the shortcut to the Taskbar, right-click on it and choose Pin to Taskbar or move the icon to the Taskbar.

The steps to link Cricut to a Windows PC are as follows:

There are two possibilities:

1. If you're using one of the Explore or Maker devices, you can *plug the USB cord* into your device or computer without having to take any additional measures.
2. If your machine and device are *Bluetooth compatible*, you can link them with Bluetooth.
    - To pair your computer using Bluetooth, go to the "Windows Settings" menu.
    - If you're not sure where to look, type "Bluetooth" into the search bar next to "Task Bar."
    - From the "Settings" menu, choose "Bluetooth & other devices" and then "Bluetooth or other devices." Bluetooth must be turned on for this to function.
    - A small dialogue box will appear on the screen. Choose "Bluetooth."
    - Choose your Cricut machine (remember it has to be on).
    - If prompted for a PIN, enter 0000 (no matter which computer you're using) and press Connect.
    - Your Cricut machine has now been connected to your device and is ready to use.

2.1.2 For MacBook

The steps to add design space on a MacBook are as follows.

- Go to design.cricut.com using an internet browser.
- To save the application to your Mac, click "download."
- The file will be downloaded and shown at the bottom of the tab. Once the download is over, click on it.
- If the file isn't showing up at the bottom of the tab, go to the "Downloads Folder" and double-click on it to begin the installation procedure.
- To begin the installation, move the Cricut icon to the Applications folder icon. Design Space for Desktop will be added to the Applications folder automatically.
- The Apps folder would open after you drag it. To start the App, go to "Cricut Design Space."
- A Mac notification can appear, asking whether you'd like to open the internet-downloaded program. To proceed, choose Open.
- Enter your Cricut Login credentials to log in.

The steps to link Cricut to a Windows MacBook are as follows:

There are two possibilities:

1. If you're using one of the Explore or Maker devices, you can *plug the USB cord* into your device or computer without having to take any additional measures.
2. If your machine and device are *Bluetooth compatible*, you can link them through Bluetooth at any time without doing any extra measures.
    - Pick "Open Bluetooth Preferences" from the "Bluetooth" icon on the top corner of your Mac.
    - It will open a little small window.
    - If your Bluetooth is turned off, enable it so that your Mac can locate your Cricut Machine.
    - As your computer appears in the Bluetooth window, pick it and press the "Connect" button.
    - If a PIN is needed, enter 0000 (no matter what computer you have) and press.
    - Your Cricut is now connected to your Mac and ready to use.

2.1.3 For iOS

To install Design Space on your iOS device,

- Launch the App Store by tapping the App Store button on your iOS device's home screen.

- Look for Cricut Design Space in the app store. The Cricut Design Space software appears as a white square in the middle with a green Cricut "C" logo.
- Tap the Get icon to download the application, and if asked, type your iTunes password to confirm the download.
- After the download is over, the application will open and give you the choice of finishing the New Device Setup or going to the App Preview.
- If you don't want to do either, press the "X" in the upper right corner to return to the landing page, sign in, and begin designing right away!

To pair/connect your Cricut machine

- Select "Bluetooth" from the "Settings" menu.
- If your Bluetooth setting is disabled, turn it on so your phone can search for your device.
- Your device would appear under "My Devices," and you can tap it to attach it to your mobile. (Don't forget to switch on your Cricut.)
- If prompted for a PIN, enter 0000.
- Return to the application to configure the computer.

2.1.4 For Android

Follow the steps below to download Cricut Design Space for Android.

- Launch the Google Play Store by tapping the Google Play Store button on your device's home screen.
- Look for Cricut Design Space in the store. The Cricut Design Space software appears as a white square in the middle with a green Cricut "C" logo.
- To download and install the software, tap the Launch tab.
- The software will show on your Application Home Screen until the installation is finished.

You must first connect your Cricut to your mobile before proceeding with the "Machine Setup." To use your Cricut unit, follow these steps:

- Pick "Device Connection" from the "Settings" menu.
- Make sure your phone is set to "Enable Bluetooth" so it can find your Cricut Machine.
- Your device may appear in the "Available Devices" section; tap it to attach it to your handset.
- If prompted for a PIN, enter 0000 (no matter which computer you're using) and press Connect.
- Return to the application to configure the computer.

2.2. Setting Up your Machine with your Cricut Account

- Once you've installed Design Space and paired it with your device, you'll need to log in before you can use it.

- Choose "Machine Setup" from the drop-down menu.
- On the Cricut Configuration, you'll be asked to choose which computer you'd like to pair.
- At this stage, you should have linked your computer to your Computer, Mac, or phone through USB or Bluetooth.
- Complete the form to generate a Cricut ID. Click "Sign Up" if you already own one.
- You can use this ID to log in to the laptop or phone application, as well as to shop for new machines and materials on Cricut.com.
- Choose "Continue."
- You may now test a cut.

2.3. Cricut access

Cricut access allows you access to the Cricut picture archive, which includes over 50,000 unlicensed photographs, over 1,000 designs, and over 400 fonts on a monthly or yearly basis.

Standard and Premium are the two different pricing options available.

- **Cricut Access (Standard)**:
  - This membership gives you access to over 500 fonts as well as over 100,000 photographs and cuts files. Furthermore, this subscription also includes a

10% discount for pictures and fonts not included with the subscription, as well as product sales.

- Cricut Access Standard subscriptions are available on a monthly or annual basis. Standard membership fees start at $7.99 a month for annual billing and $9.99 per month for regular billing. This package saves $24 for annual members!

- **Cricut Access (Premium)**:
    - The Paid membership is just as it says it is: Premium! It contains all mentioned above as well as Cricut Access, which grants Premium subscribers free Economy delivery on purchases above $50 on cricut.com as well as 20% off materials! This is a one-time payment of just under $120.

Chapter 3: Some examples of Cricut project ideas

Let's do some Cricut projects. But, before we get into the specifics of the designs, there are a few simple steps to nearly all Cricut projects.

- You'll begin by creating a design for your idea in the Design Space.
- Place your cutting mat on top of your material.
- Feed the material and tangle through the device.
- Press the cut button.
- Keep an eye on the device while it does many of the complicated tasks.
- Take the tangle out of the machine.
- Carefully remove the design.
- Remove any unwanted waste of material.
- Assemble if necessary.

3.1. Penguin Christmas card

Materials

- Reindeer Penguin
- Cardstock in occasion tints
- Silver and Red Cricut Pens
- Glue
- 12″ x 12″ Standard Grip Cricut tangle
- Cricut Explore Air 2 Cutting machine.

Instructions

- The cut patterns cling to the on-screen guidelines.
- Glue all of the penguin examples together and use craft print for topping on it, then slice out the penguin design to provide a dimensional extension to your card.
- Paste the square example at the front of the card and try to cover the square example window as far as possible.
- Cut out another inside square if desired.
- Gather the envelopes.
- Use a smaller heart as a sticker to close the envelope by pasting it to the convergence of the snowflake pattern.

3.2. Cricut Iron-On project (T-shirt making)

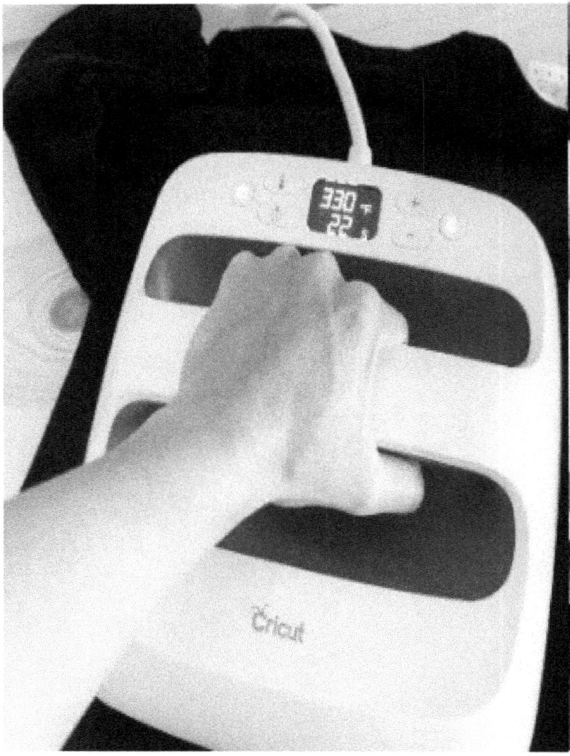

Materials

- Iron-On
- T-Shirt of your choice
- Parchment Paper
- Small Towel
- Weeder and Scraper
- Cricut EasyPress/Regular Iron
- Cricut Explore Air 2.

Instructions

- Upload the design to Cricut space.
- Weld and resize it by following the cutting instructions.
- Load Mat with Iron-On material
- Load Fine point Blade.
- Remove the pattern from the mat and weed it out.
- Transfer to a T-shirt and peel off whilst the back is still warm.
- Let it sit for 24 hours before cleaning it. Bleach should never be included.

3.3. DIY Canvas art

Materials

- Canvas
- Paint Brush
- Screwdriver
- Pliers
- Craft Knife
- Rag
- Free Downloadable Cut File
- Iron-on in Black
- Iron or Cricut EasyPress
- Staple Gun
- Wood Stain
- Weeding tools (optional)
- Cricut Machine

Instructions

- To detach the canvas from the frame, turn the canvas on to the rear and eliminate any staples keeping it in position using a screwdriver and pliers.
- Remove the cord and turn the frame around to the front. Enable to rest for a few seconds if there is some stain paint, then clean away any excess with a rag and put aside to dry entirely.
- Open Cricut Design and upload the free downloadable Cut file.

- Put the iron-on shiny side on the mat and mirror the image. The picture could then be cut.
- Clean out the extra iron-on from the edges of the words and the centers of any characters. Weeding tools make it simpler, but they're not essential.
- Position the weeded pattern on the canvas's front. Fix it with an iron or the Cricut EasyPress.
- Tear away the protective layer to expose the perfectly adhered design on the canvas.
- Fix the canvas in the frame by putting it in the middle of the stained frame and then flipping it over. Staple it to the rear of the frame in some places using a staple device.
- Cut out all of the extra canvas with a craft knife.

3.4. Infusible Ink Tote Bag

Materials

- Green StandardGrip Cricut Mat
- EasyPress 2 (or heat press)
- EasyPress 2 Mat
- Heat-resistant tape
- Tweezers

- Lint roller
- White cardstock
- Butcher paper
- Cricut Infusible Ink Blank Tote Bag
- Cricut Infusible Ink Transfer Sheet
- Cricut Explore Air 2

Instructions

- In design space, create the design. If you are designing for the first time, go for something easy like this amusing "World's Okayest Adult" badge pic.

Figure 3.5: World's Okayest Adult logo

- Reduce the scale to suit your tote. If you're using the medium EasyPress 2, it's best to render it 8.5'' x 8.5'' because you have more wiggle space along the side. In the top right corner, click Make It. Don't forget to mirror your picture when you're at the Prepare screen.

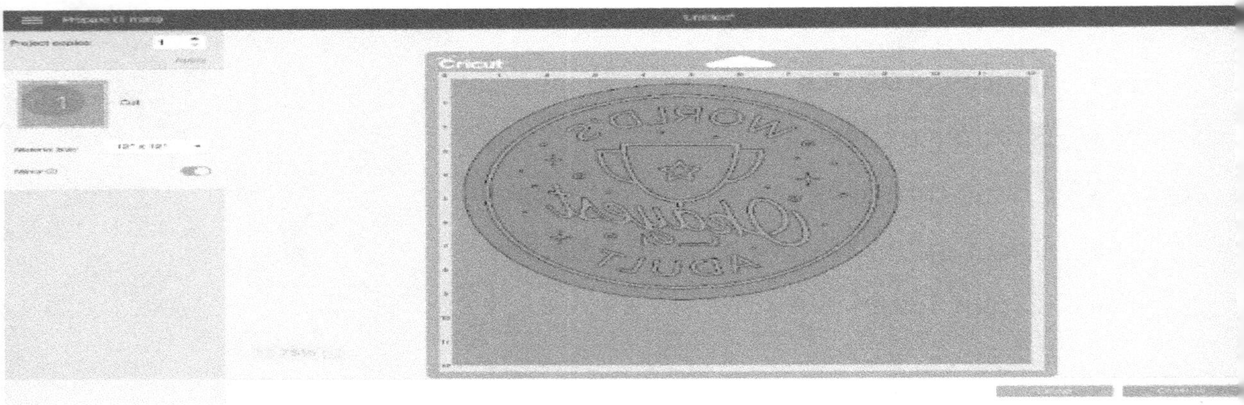

Figure 3.6: Layout Setting

- In the Make screen, use Infusible Ink Transfer Sheet should be used as your material. Be sure you're using the Fine Point Blade.

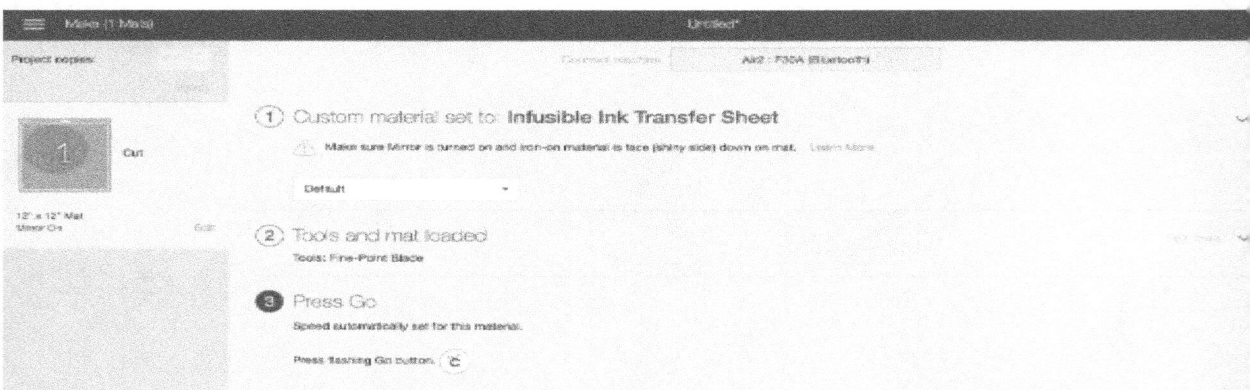

Figure 3.7: Material Setting

- Place the liner side of the sheet on the cutting pad. The sheet is extremely light grey, as you'll see! It's almost off-white in color. However, as you will note, the ink does brighten up when heated.

- Then, using Wild Rose Explore Air 2, feed it into your device and cut it out.
- Weed the infusible ink. The Infusible Ink has a paper ink sheet and a thin paper liner, similar to the dual-layer of paper.

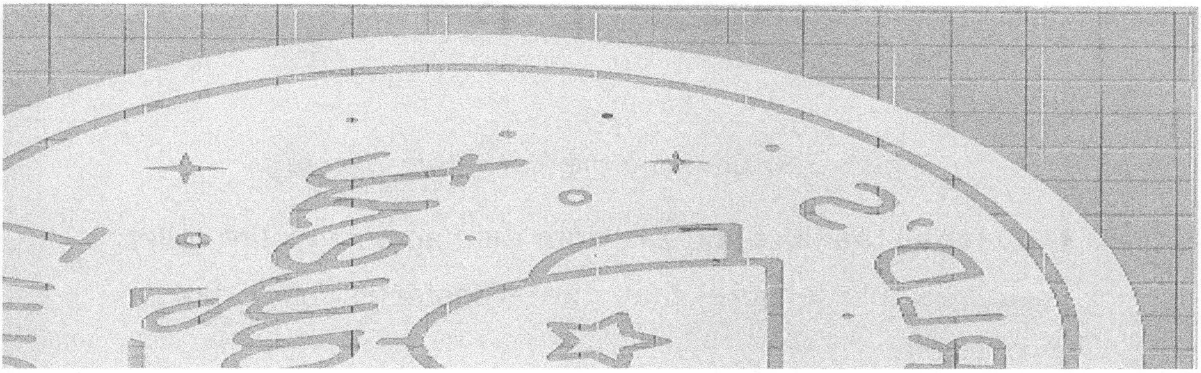

Figure 3.8: Design placement on cutting pad

- Until you begin your transfer, prepare your tote bag. Begin by placing your EasyPress Mat within a tote bag and covering it all with a white piece of cardstock. If your EasyPress mat bleeds, the cardstock will help to keep it clean.

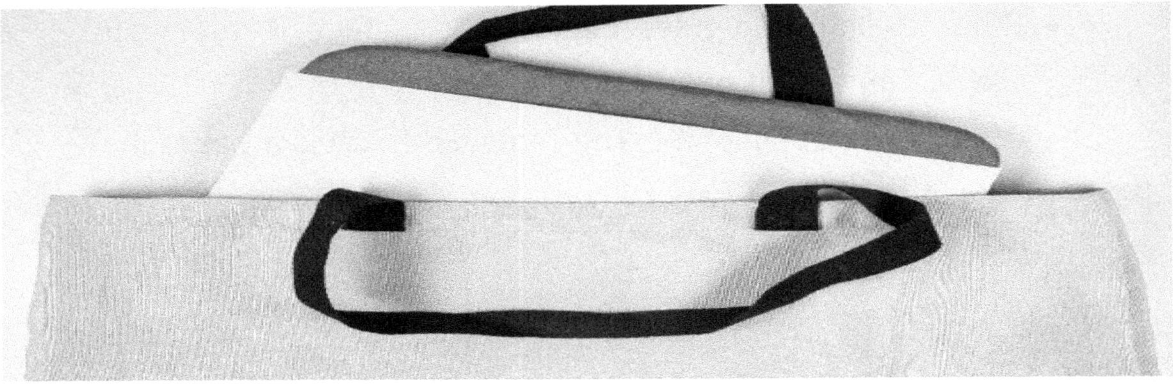

Figure 3.9: Covering the Mat within Tote bag

- Clear all the dust and dirt from the bag using a lint roller. This would ensure that the transfer is as clean as possible.

Figure 3.10: Setting up the bag.

- Move Cricut Infusible Ink with The EasyPress. Second, use butcher paper to cover your blank tote bag. To further flatten the surface and dry all moisture within the bag, pre-heat your bag before applying your switch. Allow cooling fully after pressing for 15 seconds.

Figure 3.11: Preheating

- Add your transfer after your bag has fully cooled. If you're worried about the transfer shifting, seal it with a piece of heat-resistant tape.

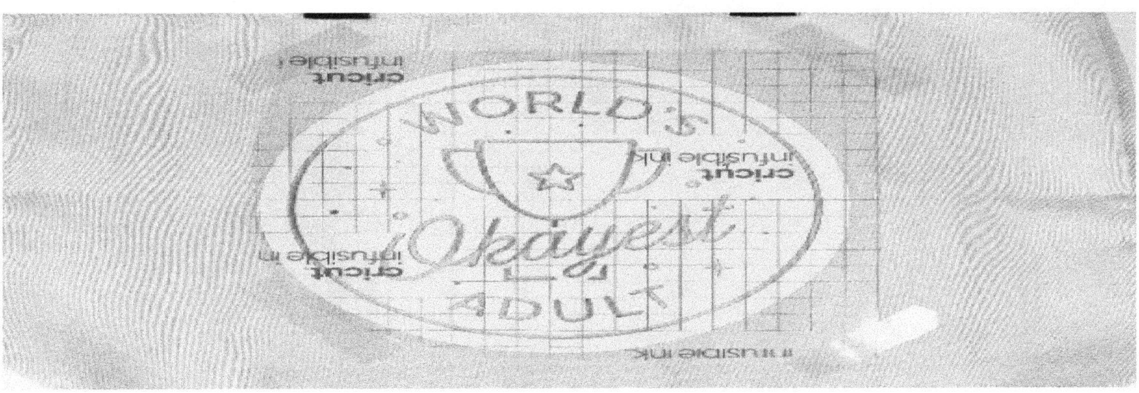

Figure 3.12: Embossing the design

- Cover the top of the transfer with butcher paper again. Then, using light but constant pressure, carefully click your EasyPress onto your design for 40 seconds. Please ensure the EasyPress is fully covering the transfer.

Figure 3.13: Infusible Ink Tote Bag

- Allow the transfer to cool until cautiously picking it up—it may not stick to your bag.

Chapter 4: Writing and Drawing with Cricut

Many of your Cricut projects, including pen and ink drawings and coloring page designs, will include hand-painted accents. Enable your Cricut machine to do the job for you if you like the style of hand-drawn art but don't want to create it yourself.

There are several unique pen colors to pick from, and a brand-new range of black pens is now available. The Cricut Pens make it simple to give your writing a more hand-drawn look.

4.1. What resources are required for drawing and writing?

Cricut machine – either of the Cricut Explore, Cricut Maker, or Cricut Joy machines should suffice.

Cricut Design Space – Using a Cricut Access account makes it easier to use the fonts and functionality. You will still use photographs and fonts from your archive instead of paying for them.

Cricut Pens - The basic fine black ink pen is included with any Cricut machine. With only this single pen, you can produce a plethora of fantastic designs. Different types of Cricut pens are listed below:

- **Fine tip pens** are available in a variety of colors. These are ideal for applying accents to your artwork. The tips are tiny enough to illustrate minor details while maintaining a clean line. In general, 0.3 and 0.4 sizes are ideal for about anything.
- **Calligraphy pens** are available in a range of styles, including up to two calligraphy pen nib size range. This will encourage you to use your Cricut pen art to make a fancy calligraphy look.
- **Glitter pens** resembles ballpoint pens and with a smooth paint glide to the paint, resulting in a colorful glitter effect with a clear pattern.
- **Metallic pens** normally have a much larger tip and draw in a similar manner to a medium size marker.

4.2. The Cricut Writing tool Palette

Simply mark the line as "draw" in the Design space to produce a painting or writing line. To do so, follow these steps:

- Choose the picture layer from which you like to illustrate. If it's a pen, scissors, or scanner, click the layer icon. The palette would appear, allowing you to choose "draw". After that, you can also select a color for that project layer.
- You have the option of selecting the color where you'd like your design to appear on display. If all the pictures needed to be sketched using the identical black pen, for example, choose the same paint as well as pen for each style in your final piece.
- You'll be prompted to adjust your pen colors as required when you configure Cricut to build your model inside Design Space. Any color you choose can result in a notification telling you when to change your tool color when Cricut is working on it.

4.3. Drawing Projects

4.3.1 What are the steps to creating your own butterfly coloring page?

Materials

- White Cardstock
- Butterfly SVG design by Jen Goode
- Colored pencils (optional)
- Cricut Pen
- Cricut machine (Explore, Air or Maker)

Instructions

- Open Cricut Design Space and upload the butterfly design.
- All of the layers should be set to drawing/writing. To make complete designs, group the like pieces together. Each wing has its own design layer; you can join all four parts together to make a group or "weld" them together to make a single item.
- To make the picture you like, move the designs around.
- You may make several butterflies by duplicating bits. To build different looks, add extra parts to certain butterflies and layer separate draw lines.
- If you've found a style you want, pick the whole canvas (everything) and join all of the elements into a single package. Once you move to the "create it" mat, this will keep the whole design in position.

- Create it by pressing the "make it" button and following the on-screen directions.

4.3.2 How to print, cut and draw with your Cricut.

Materials

- Paper
- Cricut pens
- Printer synced with your Cricut.
- Cricut cutting machine – any version will work.
- Cricut Design Space

Instructions

- Select the appropriate design.
- Attach the printed painting and the drawing together.
- Use a range of drawing patterns to complement the printed designs. Here are few suggestions:
- Add a shiny drawing touch to written picture borders or outlines. In Cricut Design Room, duplicate the outline of a printed picture and transform it into a drawing or writing. Until sending the project to the mat, apply the line to the written form.
- Convert a few of the cut elements into drawing lines to give the designs a special look. Since you can't flatten a drawing line, make sure you flatten any of the written bits before attaching the drawing line.
- To add a finishing touch, add additional drawing accents like boundaries or lines to the final printed parts.
- Create art drawing patterns with Cricut.

4.3.3 Use the Cricut to build layered designs

When you want to make hand-drawn artwork with your Cricut, but the designs don't go together well, making paper layers will help. Certain art designs make for several layers, whilst others do not, so pay attention to the designs you choose to create with layers.

- **What are the requirements for creating layered designs?**
    - Layered draw designs have to have a cut and a draw/write line. You'll need to search for art that either allows you to cut around the painting or can be edited to allow you to cut across the drawing line.
- **Creating cut layers**
    - Many of the art files have different layers for the design, such that cutting and painting can be done. This isn't the case for all art. To make layered draw art, you will need to build your own cut layers sometimes.

Figure 4.1: Creating cut layers.

  - If the art you choose to use doesn't have these separate layers, you'll have to make them yourself or choose another piece of art. Here's an explanation (*figure 4.2)* of what you might be looking for. Each section of the ice cream cone has its own layer. As desired, you can alter each layer separately.

- **Editing draw layers**
  - You may choose to create a design but not have all of the specifications, or you may want to adjust the colors used in various aspects of the design. For this, use contour. The Contour function may be used to edit several drawing styles. Simply pick the layer you would like to update, press Contour, and then cover the parts of the drawing you don't want to create.

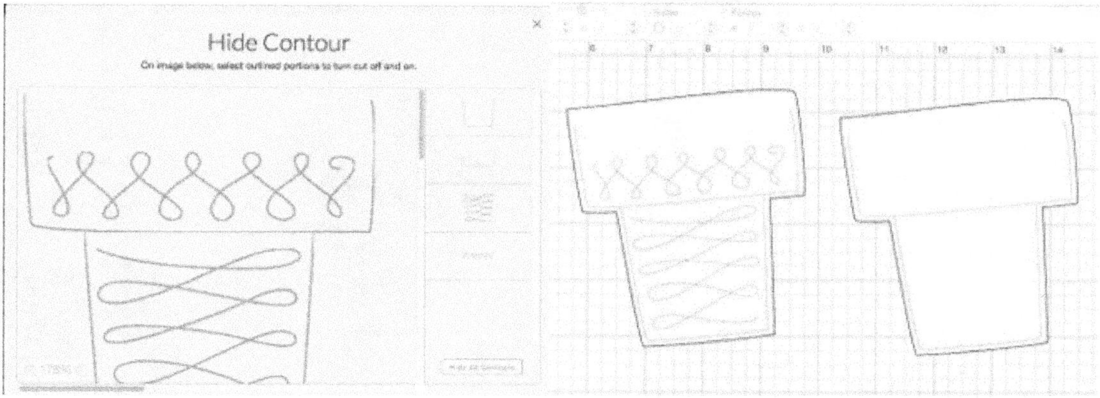

Figure 4.2: Editing with Contour function

- **Attaching drawn art to each layer**
  - Draw and write lines must always be connected to a cut shape; otherwise, they will simply draw on the page and will not be cut off. You don't need to attach anything if you have a card and just wish to write on it. For all other times, make sure the draw lines are still connected to the shape you expect them to be drawn on.

Figure 4.3: colored and uncolored artwork

- In certain instances, you will flatten all of the layers and then sketch on the flattened artwork as well. Experiment with the different solutions to see which one fits well with the project you're working on. Use various shades of paper to add painting effects, or only use plain white paper to draw the star. Here's an example (Figure 4.4) of the same artwork in both colored and uncolored versions.

Chapter 5: Cricut Project Ideas

There are about as many Cricut ideas as there are humans, multiplied by the materials available. You can make great DIY crafts for every purpose with a Cricut Maker, Cricut Explore, or the adorable Cricut Joy.

Let's have a look at several projects that range from simple to difficult.

5.1. Tassels

Tassels may be used in a variety of ways. These are extremely simple to produce and can be made to fit any task. Use them as a keyring or zipper pick, add them to the sides of pillows or covers, hang them from a rope to create a banner, and a thousand other items! You may even make them out of leather or faux leather for a more elegant look. Tassels look great on almost everything.

smiles today

Materials

- Fabric mat
- 12" x 18" fabric rectangles
- Glue gun
- Cricut machine

Instructions

- Launch Design Space to begin a new design.
- Click the "Image" icon in the bottom left-hand corner and type "tassel" into the search box.
- Press "Insert" after selecting the illustration of a rectangle with lines on either side.
- Arrange fabric on the mat and use the Cricut to cut out the pattern.
- Take the fabric off the mat and save the excess square.
- Beginning from the uncut side, position the material face down and roll tightly. As required, untangle the fringe.
- To attach the tassel at the top, use some waste fabric and a hot glue stick.
- Use your beautiful tassels to decorate anything you like!

5.2. Paw Print Socks

Socks are the epitome of comfort. Small paw prints add a cool, secret decoration to the base of your socks. Every time you cuddle up, show off your affection towards pets. You can do this with about every small style or even add text to the base of your foot to add a quotation. You can select any kind of socks you choose. Please ensure the sock and vinyl colors contrast for easy reading. Or, for a hidden design, make them all in the same color! Under certain lighting, the vinyl shine will contrast with the fabric. You'll require your Cricut EasyPress or iron for this since it uses heat transfer vinyl.

Materials

- Socks
- Weeding tool or pick
- Scrap cardboard
- Heat transfer vinyl
- Cutting mat
- Cricut EasyPress or iron
- Cricut machine

Instructions

- Build a new project in Cricut Design Space.
- Check for "paw prints" using the "Photo" button in the bottom left-hand corner.
- Select your preferred paw prints and click "Insert."
- Send the pattern to the Cricut by placing the iron-on material on the mat.
- To eliminate excess material, use a pick or weeding tool.
- Take the material from the mat and stuff the socks with scrap cardboard.
- Put the iron-on material onto the socks' bottoms.
- To attach it to the iron-on material, use EasyPress.
- Take the cardboard from the socks after they have cooled.
- Put on your adorable paw print socks!

5.3. Monogrammed Drawstring Bag

Drawstring bags are simple to use and carry. They're just as easy to produce as they are to use! These bags can be kept on hand for anyone in your family to pick and go as required. You may use monograms to distinguish them, or you can use a different pattern on each one to modify it for a certain purpose or simply to decorate it. This can also be used as gift bags! The designs are made of heat transfer vinyl, so you'll need your Cricut EasyPress or iron for this project.

Hair
Stuff

Materials

- Heat transfer vinyl
- Two matching rectangles of fabric
- Weeding tool or pick
- Cutting mat
- Needle and thread
- Ribbon
- Cricut machine
- Cricut EasyPress or iron

Instructions

- Build a new project in Cricut Design Space.
- Check for "monogram" using the "Image" icon in the bottom left-hand corner.
- Select the monogram you want to use and press "Insert."
- Place the shiny liner side of the iron-on material on the mat and give the pattern to the Cricut.
- To eliminate excess material, use the weeding tool or a pick.
- Remove the monogram out of the mat.
- The monogram should be centered on your material and moved down a couple of inches, so it doesn't get rolled up as the ribbon is created.
- The pattern should be ironed onto the fabric.
- Put the two rectangles along such that the fabric's outside side is faced inward.

- Leave a seam allowance when you sew along with the corners. Let the top open and stop it a few inches below the top.
- Fold the bag's top back until the stitches are reached.
- Sew around the folded edge's bottom, keeping the sides open.
- Turn bag's right side out.
- The ribbon should be threaded through the loop at the top of the bag.
- Bring what you need in your fresh drawstring pocket!

5.4. Customized Pillow

A simple concept that is often requested and quick to personalize. Make the pillow of your dreams!

STEWART
EST. 1998

Materials

- Insert Cricut Access
- Protective Sheet Pillow Cover
- Glitter Iron-On Vinyl
- Iron-On
- Cricut Easypress Mat
- Cricut Machine

Instructions

- From the Home tab of the Cricut Design Space, select "New Project."
- Click the text icon in the lower right corner of the page and choose the font you like. Fill in your name and adjust the size of the box corner to fit your pillow.
- To add an additional bit of text for your Est. Year, choose the Text button. Drag and arrange your last name properly.
- Choose all textboxes at the same time and hit the attach button. It will link the two text boxes, allowing for precise cutting.
- The screen appears as you click the "Make It" icon. Allow that the Mirror is turned on.
- To switch on and off the mirror setting, click the image in the upper left corner. The image above appears on the computer. Turn the "off" switch on.

- Press the Mirror button; the mat will now reflect your mirrored image, and you're ready to load your Iron-On Vinyl shiny side down onto your mat. Follow the instructions by clicking and dragging.
- Weed the excess vinyl and center the pillow cover design once the design has been sliced.
- Use the Easypress Settings Chart to set the timer and temperature for your material.
- Use the Iron-On Protection Sheet to cover the structure, then top it with the Easypress and press the Cricut button. When it has beeped, remove it. Heat for 10 to 15 seconds on the other side of your pillow cover.
- Enable the iron-on to cool before removing the sheet.

5.5. Cricut Gift Boxes

What is the point of creating crafts if you don't gift them? You may even create your own box designs after you've become more comfortable with the Design Space software – nothing beats training for honing a talent. Let's have a look at how you should get started designing your own gift

boxes right now.

Materials

- Scoring wheel
- Cardstock (Glitter or of your choice)
- Glue
- Cricut machine

Instructions

- Launch Cricut Design Space and choose "New Project," then import the SVG file patterns you've searched or downloaded. Alternately, start creating your own box patterns.
- Start with the pillowcase package, which is probably the easiest to create for a novice. Using the upper formatting panel in Design Space, resize the patterns to suit the box's expected size. If you're producing more than one box, make sure to click "Ungroup" to distinguish the prototypes that need to be cut and assembled separately. Before submitting the design to cutting, make sure to adjust the Line form to "Score" for any sections of the model that should be folded. After you've finished scoring the lines which have to be folded, pick the whole pattern and click on "Attach," then finish sizing, if necessary, before clicking "Make it."
- When deciding on cutting settings under "Make it," use cardstock as your chosen material. You should start

cutting after you've arranged the material and the cutting pad.

- Assemble the box(es) you'll be using. You won't need to use adhesive to hold the pieces of the box intact if you use light materials like paper or standard cardstock. If you're using glitter cardstock or similar materials, though, you'll need to glue all of the pieces of the package together except the portion that's meant to seal it.
- Begin putting together your package, gluing the pieces that need to be sealed while you move. To help it go smoother and more efficiently, use tacky glue or a glue gun. And your box is all set!

5.6. Personalized Christmas Ornaments

Merry Christmas y'all
All is Bright

Materials

- Heat-Resistant Tape
- Cardstock (white)
- Sublimation Ornaments in Blank Form
- Butcher paper
- Mat and EasyPress 2
- Explore Air 2 Machine or Cricut Maker
- Buffalo Check Cricut Infusible Ink Transfer Sheet
- Cloth without any lint

Instructions

- Create your own personalized holiday ornaments by starting a new design in Cricut Design Space.
- For the front and back of each ornament, place two 2.81'' circles. Using the slice feature to generate negative space photographs of the designs within the circle after adding your favorite holiday photos and custom text to the circle.
- Cut your designs with your Cricut machine (ensure to mirror your picture before cutting!) and weed the unwanted Infusible Ink with your fingertips or tweezers.
- Remove any dust, dirt, or smudges from the ornament's surface with a lint-free fabric.
- Apply Infusible Ink on both sections of the blank ornament and cover with heat-resistant tape.

- Preheat the EasyPress 2 to 400°F and set the timer for 240 seconds. Cover with another layer of butcher paper after placing the ornaments on top of the butcher paper.
- Place the EasyPress 2 on top of the decorations for 240 seconds; just don't press down! Place the EasyPress 2 back on its base after the loop is over, then carefully peel the top layer of butcher paper.

5.7 Christmas Tea Towels

Christmas tea towels are a simple and quick way to get started with the Cricut cutting unit. Simply use heat transfer vinyl to provide almost limitless design options.

Materials

- Tea towel with a deer silhouette
- Tea towel "Merry and Bright."
- flour sack towels (white)
- Cut files and iron-on for Christmas tea towels.
- Tool for weeding
- press cloth or parchment paper.
- Iron or EasyPress
- Cricut Explore Air 2 or Cricut Maker

Instructions

- In Design Space, open the Christmas tea towel cut file(s).
- Adjust the sizes and colors to your liking. Don't neglect to mirror the text while cutting the iron-on vinyl for your Christmas tea towels.
- Choose the materials. The cutting material on the Cricut Maker is selected directly in Design Space; many of the most popular cutting material choices may appear.
- With the weeder unit, remove any negative space from the designs.
- Place the patterns on the towel with the liners and see where you like them.

- Set the EasyPress's temperature and timer according to the instructions for the material you're ironing on and the material you're ironing on to. Preheat the tea towel by ironing it to prevent any wrinkles. Cover the pattern with the press cloth or parchment paper and press down tightly for the period shown on the map. To begin the timer, press the right-hand Cricut button. Enable the liners to cool down for a moment after the timer goes off before trying to peel them off. Replace the filler and click for another 5–10 seconds if some aspect of the pattern starts to pull up.

Chapter 6: How to make Paper projects with Cricut?

Paper is readily available and offered in a wide variety of colors, textures, sizes, and finishes. It has many applications. The options are endless when it comes to cards, drawings, and custom designs. A few of the most common Paper Projects will be discussed in this chapter.

6.1 Paper Flowers

Flowers are lovely, but they don't last long until they wilt. However, paper ones will last you forever! It can be used as decoration for an event or gathering. Brides on a budget will also use this instead of an extravagant flower arrangement to walk down the aisle! In the Cricut Design Space, you'll find a plethora of flower models. You can also look for more on the internet or try your hand at designing your own. A bouquet may consist of a single form of a flower, the same flower in various colors, a combination of flowers, or a variation of flowers in the same color. It all relies on the feel and look you want to achieve, so go for which approach appeals to you.

Materials

- Light Grip Mat
- Card Stock Paper
- Adhesive
- Cricut Air 2 Machine

Instructions

- In Design Space, enter "Flower" in the Search Field. There are several flower options; most will perform as long as they have a stable center. It is entirely up to you to make your decision!
- Open the project while selecting the flower that you like.

- Copy and paste flower (5 times), making each flower shorter than the last when you paste it in place. This will give the final product complexity and texture by creating different sizes. Make sure your Cricut machine is set to cardstock after you've posted all of the flower designs.
- A paper should be lined up according to the layout/mat.
- Submit the Project for Cutting
- Remove and gently lift Flowers from the Mat.
- Cut flowers can be lined up in order of size, from largest to smallest, so they can be stacked.
- Petals should be bent upwards from the middle. Start with the largest paper flower and work your way through the other four, twisting each one a little further each time.
- Using your adhesive, glue the flowers together. Position the flowers on top of each other, beginning from the largest flower and working the way down to the smallest.

6.2 Coffee Cup Gift Card Holder

Materials

- LightGrip Mat
- Cardstock
- Your gift card
- Corrugated cardboard
- SVG design
- Tacky glue
- A pen
- Cricut Maker cutting machine, Cricut Explore or Cricut Joy

Instructions

- Open Cricut Design Space and import the coffee cup (gift card holder) SVG cut file.
- Place your materials on the LightGrip cutting pad, choose the appropriate cutting substance, load your blade as instructed, and cut your pattern.
- Take all of the material from the Mat.
- Attach the lid to the inner cup's top.
- You may either insert the gift card into the slits or glue it into the cardholder bag. To use the pocket, lay the card pocket face down, position your gift card on top of it, and properly glue around it, as seen in the picture below. Pick up the pocket and card and put them together on your inner cup, pressing down.

- Fold the outer cup sheet in half and glue the lower part of the outer cup, as well as one of the outer cup's edges. Fold the paper back up and hold it until the glue is dry.
- Fold the wrapping over the outside of the cup and glue all edges.
- On the sticker, write the recipient's name. Glue the top and bottom labels together, then to the wrap. Your cup is all set!

6.3 Paper Butterfly Bouquet

Materials

- Flower stem wire
- 2-by-12-inch cardstock in multiple colors
- 1 Cricut 12-by-12-inch LightGrip Adhesive Cutting Mat
- Cricut Explore Air 2

Instructions

- Upload the design you've chosen to Design Space. Click "Customize" to update the project, then use the options in the Edit bar to make improvements. Click "Make It" or "Continue."
- Using the StandardGrip pad, position the first piece of cardstock. To load the machine, follow these instructions: Select "Cardstock" on the SmartSet Dial. Clamp B should be loaded with a fine-point razor. Click the "Load / Unload" button after loading the Mat.
- Cut by pressing the blinking "Go" icon. Remove the Mat. Remove the wasted material, then raise the individual butterflies with the spatula from the simple toolset if necessary.
- Repeat the above step when Load each fresh sheet of cardstock onto the cutting pad, then feed it into the machine as directed.
- Sort the butterfly pieces into groups based on color and shape.

- To make the butterflies double-sided, hot glue the contrasting bits together.
- Attach all the butterflies to a piece of decorative stem string or floral wire.
- Arrange the flower wires in your hand before placing them in a vase. (For a more comfortable catch, use decorative foam in your vessel).

Chapter 7: Tips And Trick

Using a Cricut is a thrilling experience. For a novice, it may even be intimidating and daunting. These 28 Cricut Tricks and Secrets can save your sanity and help you remain more organized along the way, whether you're a newcomer or a professional Cricut crafter.

7.1 Cricut Tricks and Secrets

2. Peel the mat instead of material

While it can sound natural to peel the material (vinyl, cardstock, etc.) away from the surface, it is simply preferable to softly curl and peel the mat away from the stuff. This helps to save the art supplies from being so distorted.

2. For vinyl storage, use IKEA plastic bags.

IKEA plastic bag storage holders are another favorite Cricut hacks that have gained some attention in recent years. They're great for keeping vinyl rolls. You can even get some on the internet!

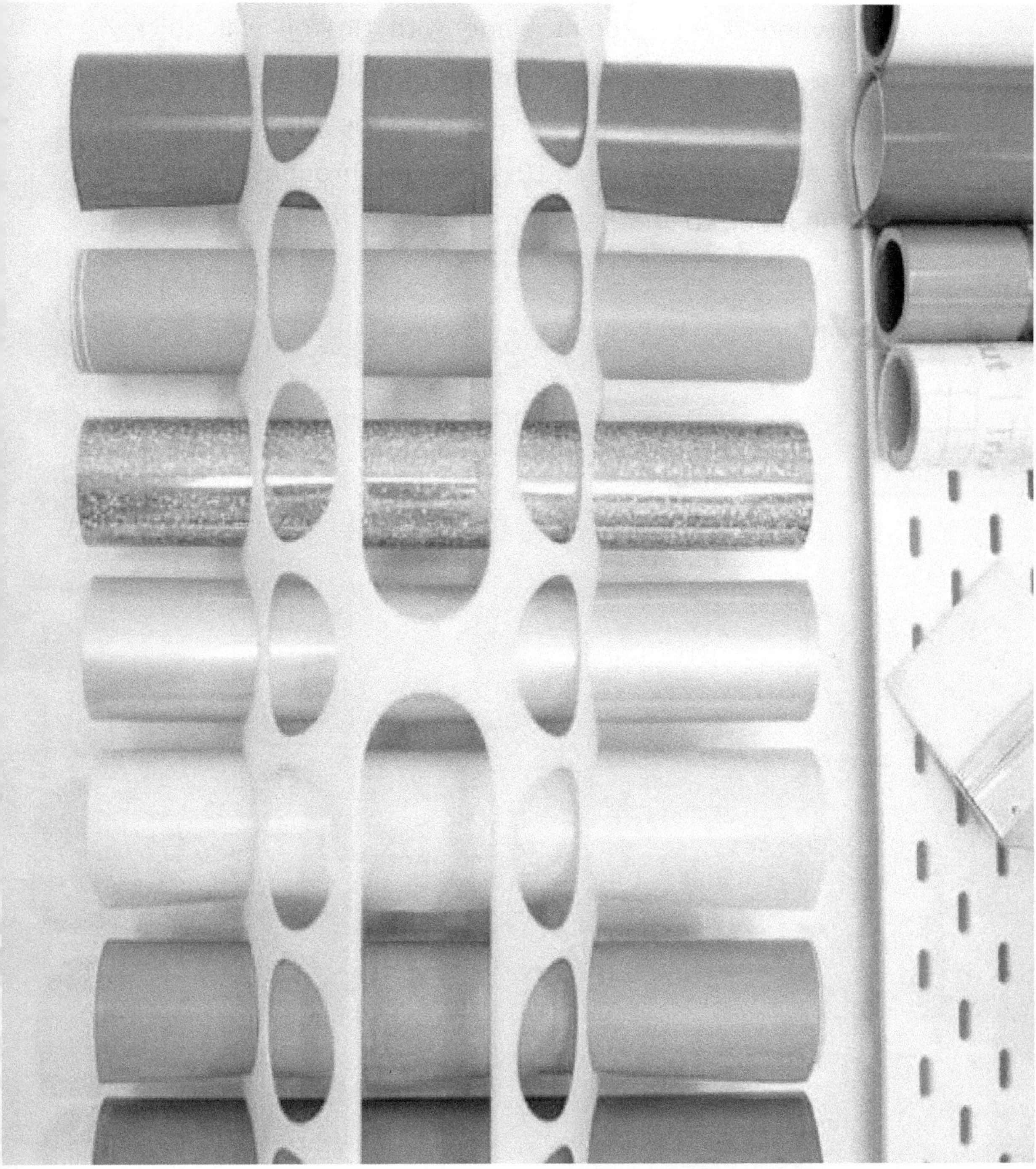

3. Tin foil should be used to sharpen the razor.

Sharpening the fine-point blade with tin foil will quickly prolong its life! In reality, using tin foil will extend the blade's life by three times! Remove the blade from the clamp and pass the edge 10-12 times through the tin foil with the blade to sharpen it.

4. keep your knives in the Cricut.

This could seem self-evident, but as a novice Cricut user, you may have no idea that the interior of your system could store the blades and small tools in a dust-free, secure manner.

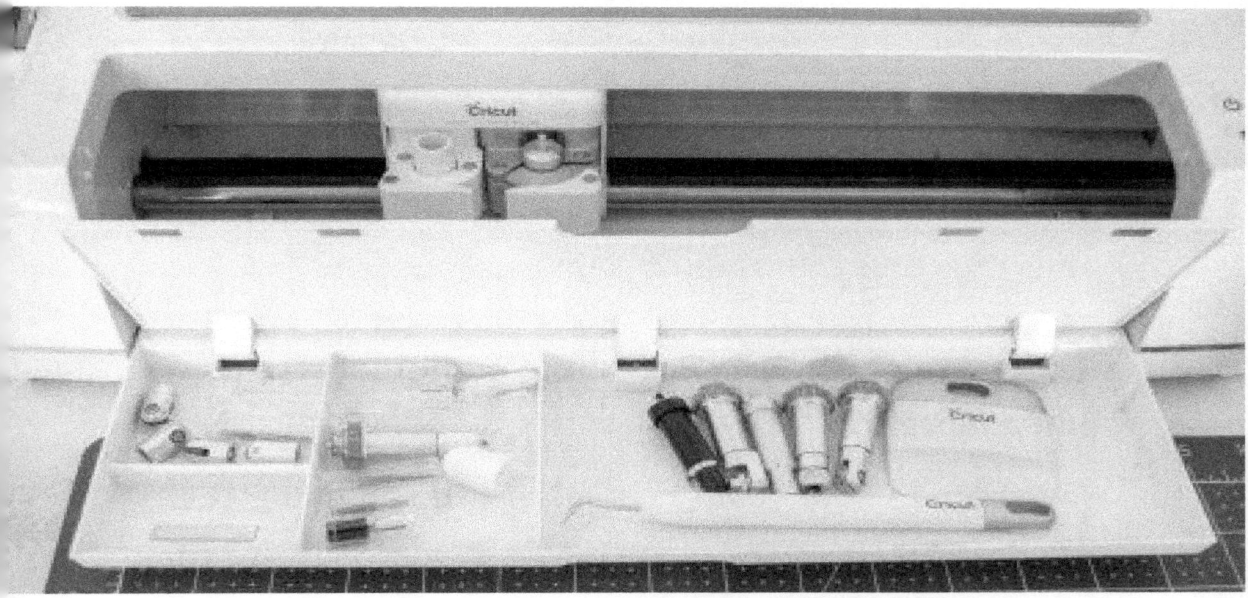

5. Pick up little fragments from your pad or pattern with a lint roller (Works for glitter too)

You should quickly catch the excess little bits on a lint roller if you have an elaborate pattern cut out on paper or vinyl to save time!

It's still great for picking up stray glitter on your desk.

6. In spite of using Cricut pens for your laptop, use pen adapters.

The ability to have your Cricut machine compose for you is a fantastic function. You'll actually wish you could use pens rather than Cricut pens at some stage.

The good news is that if you have an Explore 2 or later, you can buy pen adapters that will enable you to use almost any brand of a pen! Sharpies, brush pens, and more are all available!

How to Use ALL these Pens with Your Cricut!
1. Sharpie Fine Point
2. Sharpie Ultra Fine Point
3. Sharpie Pen Art Pen
4. Pilot Precise
5. Bic Marking
6. Bic Cristal
7. Sakura Gelly Roll
8. Amaza Gel Pens
9. Sharpie Oil-Based Paint
10. Uni-ball Signo UM-153
11. Crayola Fine Line Marker
12. Crayola Super Tip
13. Crayola Detailing Gel Pen
14. Tombow Duel Brush Pens

7. For vinyl remnants, use a nail polish tray.

One of most favorite Cricut hacks is this one! When weeding, get a cheap nail polish holder to catch tiny vinyl bits.

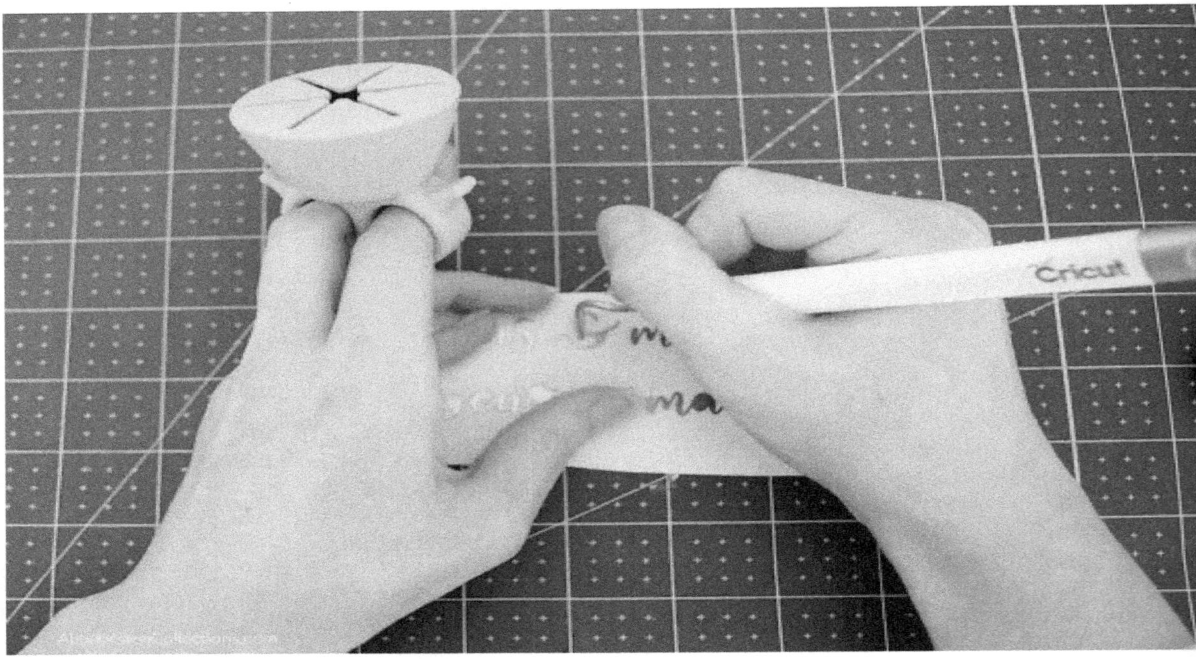

8. Inkscape is a free program that allows you to create your own SVG cut files.

SVG files for Design Space can be found for free or purchased by Cricut Access. So what if you had your own?

After all, there are occasions when there is a need to introduce a specific vision to life or customize an object. Inkscape is a free, open-source software for creating SVG files from nothing or converting images to layered SVG files.

9. Converting a picture to an SVG is as simple as clicking a button

If you aren't ready to learn how to build your own SVG files, use the one-click picture to SVG converter instead.

10. Use a pegboard to keep all of your Cricut materials organized

Pegboards are vital for keeping supplies ordered, and you can save money by using unused wall space! These can be used at Amazon or on IKEA. Plus, Cricut hacks like this really help to make your craft room look nice.

11. Baby wipes may be used to clean your mat. Resticky the mat with Easy Tack

Cleaning the dirt off of recycled Cricut mats with baby wipes will give them a new lease on existence. You may even re-sticky every mat for another 5-10 uses by spraying it with a few coats of Easy Tack.

12. To hold vinyl rolls tight, use slap bracelets.

If you have a lot of vinyl, then keep the rolls in a variety of places. Slap bracelets are an inexpensive way to keep vinyl rolls intact.

13. Sort the vinyl into wood bins by type.

It's important to keep track of your vinyl styles (iron-on, textured, adhesive, etc.). Bins may be a convenient way to organize items by category and mark each bin for easy identification.

14. Trim vinyl with a smooth edge to prevent rough corners.

If you're not patient, vinyl is one of the materials that can easily be thrown away. Trimming the vinyl before cutting can help hold the edges straight and reduce waste.

15. Discover fantastic SVG freebies

Free SVG files for Design Space can be listed on Pinterest searches, among other sites. There is a huge Freebie Vault at Abbi Kirsten Collections of over 150 free SVG and printable models!

16. For tougher fabrics, use painter's tape

Painters tape will be your best buddy if your things are rolling around on your mat. It's particularly relevant when working with wood and chipboard.

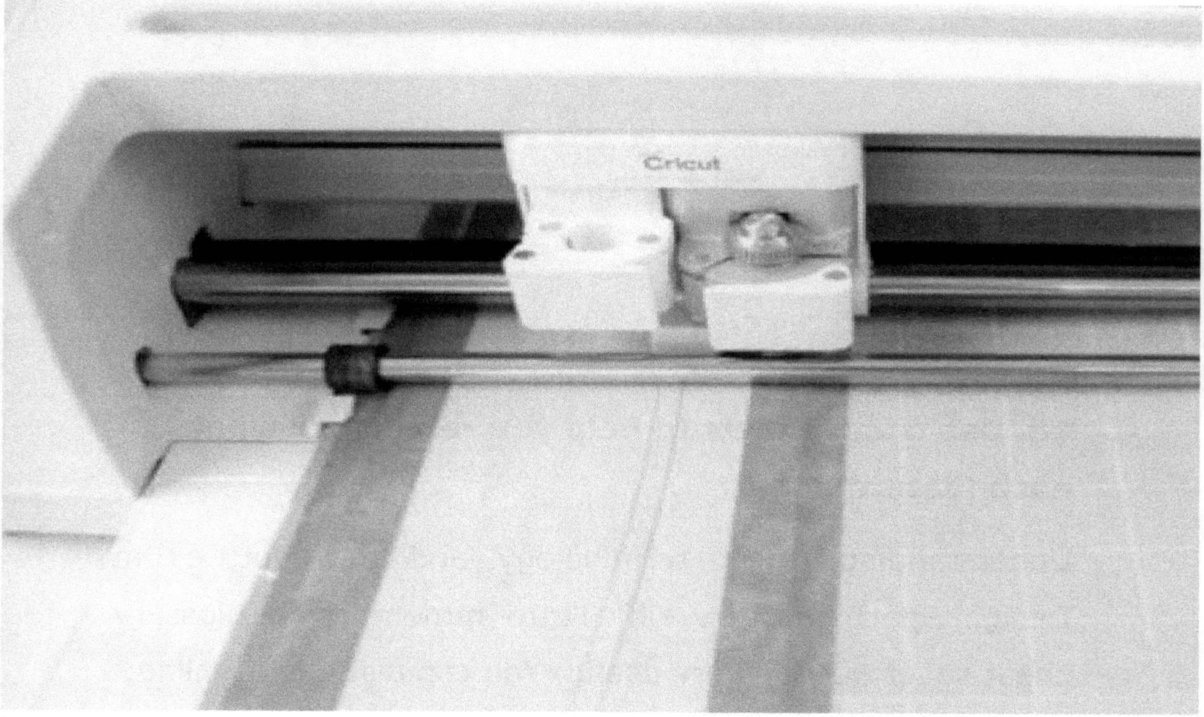

17. When adding vinyl to angled surfaces, cut slits in the transfer tape.

On a curved wall, how can you get the vinyl to be smooth?

Aside from practice, one technique is to make slits along the edges of the transfer tape. This gives the tape some wiggle room when you position the pattern.

18. Use cheat sheets to help you remember what each feature does.

Understanding Cricut terminology and the features in Design Space may be difficult to remember; a glossary cheat sheet may be very useful. You can also get it online.

19. Use a magazine holder to store vinyl remnants.

Don't throw out the odd and ends of vinyl! Small cuts can also be made for them. To see what you have to deal from, keep your scraps in a plain magazine holder.

20. Make use of a printable environment guide

Trying to recall any of those content settings or custom settings, much as Design Space features is almost difficult! There is a free guide on the subject that you can find inside the Freebie Vault!

21. On wood, use iron-on vinyl (HTV).

Well, indeed! Iron-on vinyl should be used on wood! To make it easier, Cricut has heat guidance. The look of heat transfer vinyl to that of adhesive vinyl is preferred mostly.

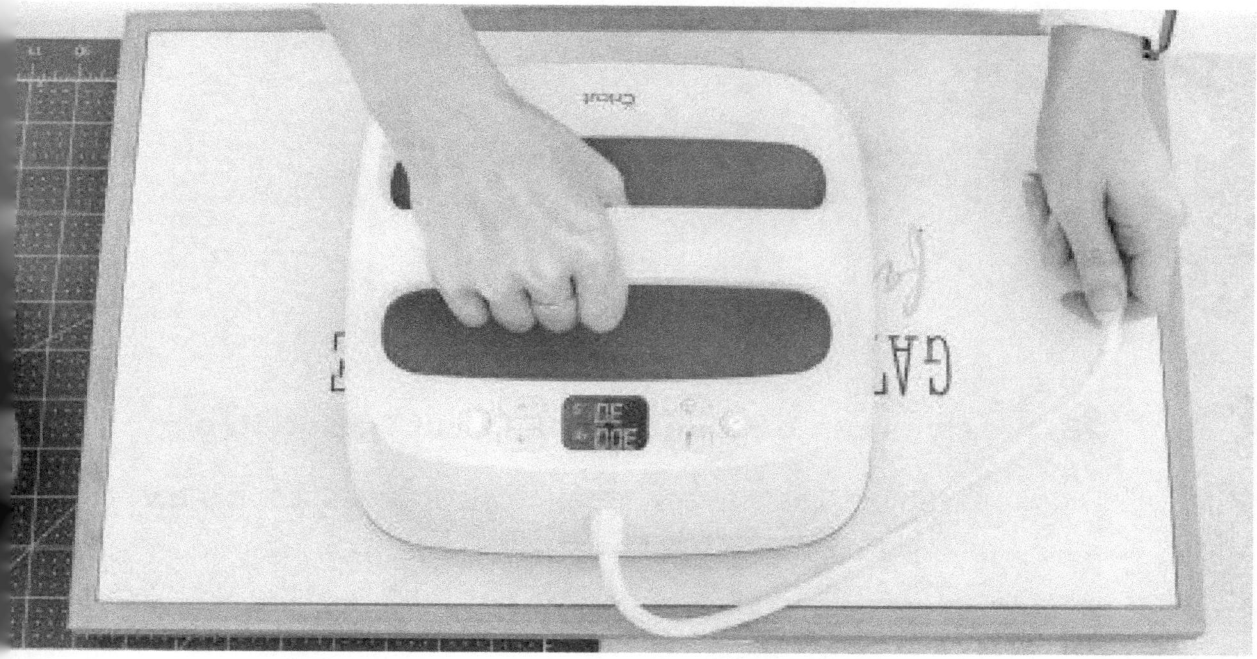

22. Use the Cricut Easy Mini-Press to apply iron-on vinyl to tumblers.

In 2019, Cricut launched the Easypress Micro, a miniature variant of the Easypress. This little gadget is so adorable and useful that it also allows you to iron on vinyl to your tumblers!

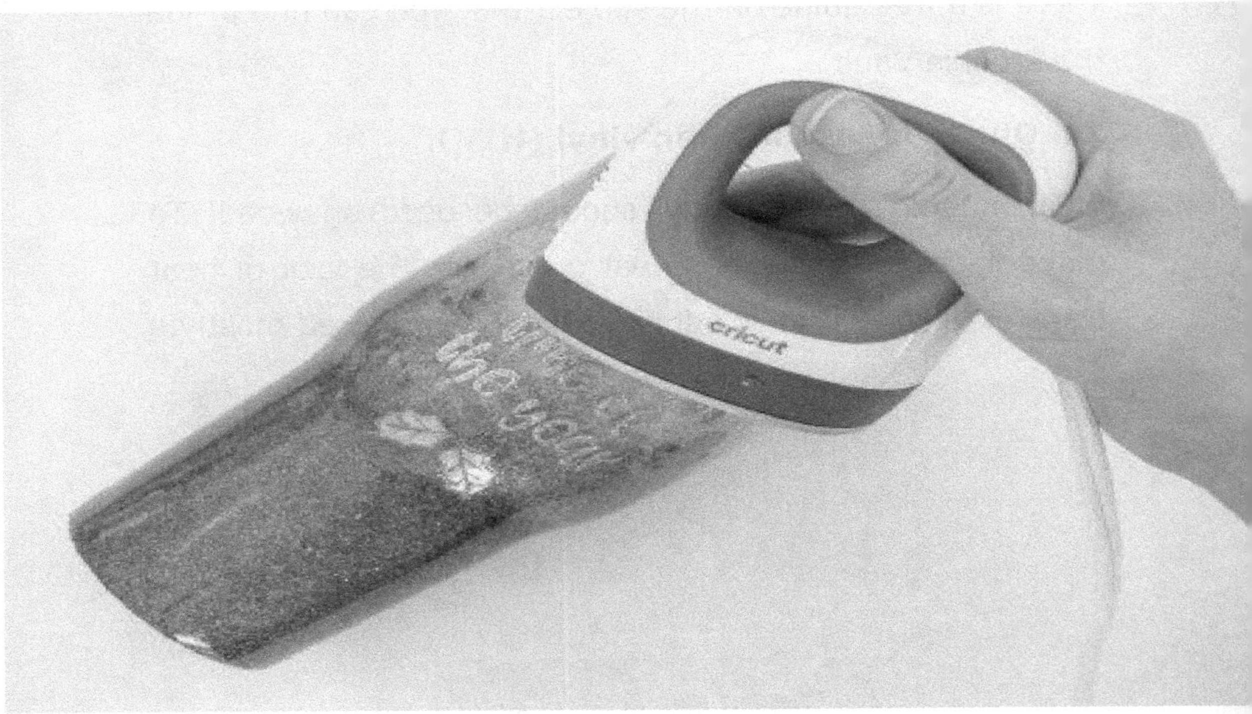

23. Freebies can be found in the Cricut Design Room.

Did you realize that every week, Cricut releases a new package of freebies that anybody can use, even if they don't have Cricut Access?! Freebies can be found under Images > Filter > Freebies!

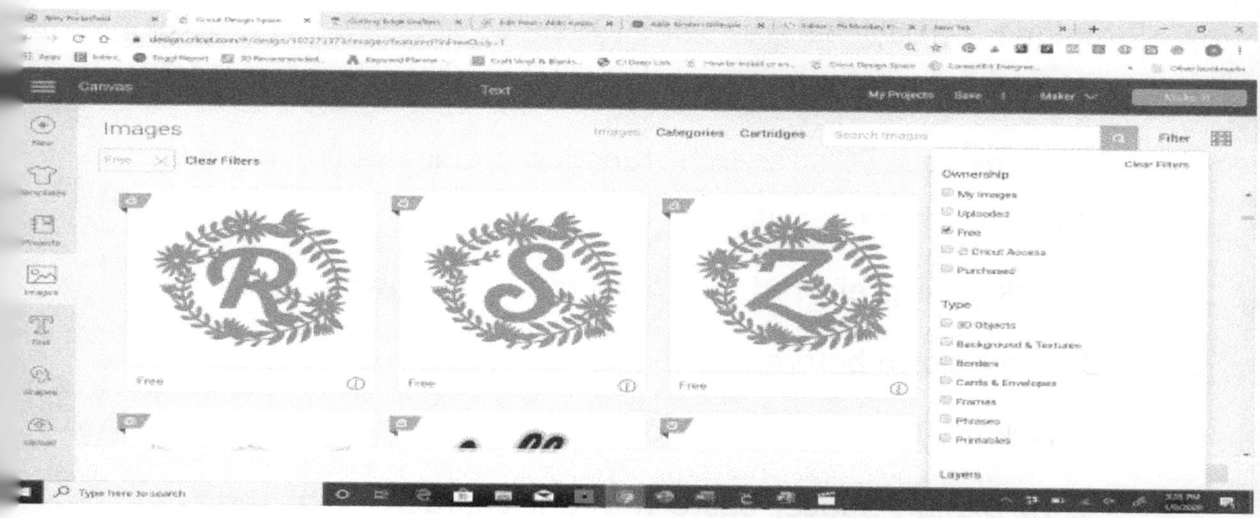

24. Understand where to look for the right fabrics

It can take a long time and a lot of trial and error to figure out where to find the best-priced Cricut products. You can take help from the internet regarding this.

25. Use the internet to find free fonts.

You're losing out if you haven't yet mastered the strength of downloading free fonts for your Cricut. Check out the internet for the top 60 free and paid fonts, as well as exclusive Christmas font posts!

26. Import specialty projects to build a room using character maps

It's one thing to download fonts, but it's quite another to learn how to make a word appear like a million bucks! It took me a while to figure out that you can navigate those unique scrolly letters using your computer's "character charts" or "glyphs."

1. Go to your PC's "search" function and look for "character map" or "character viewer" on the Mac.

2. Pick your preferred font from the drop-down menu.

3. Scroll down before you reach the letter you're looking for.

4. Pick it with a click, then copy it.

5. In Design Space, paste the font character into the text box.

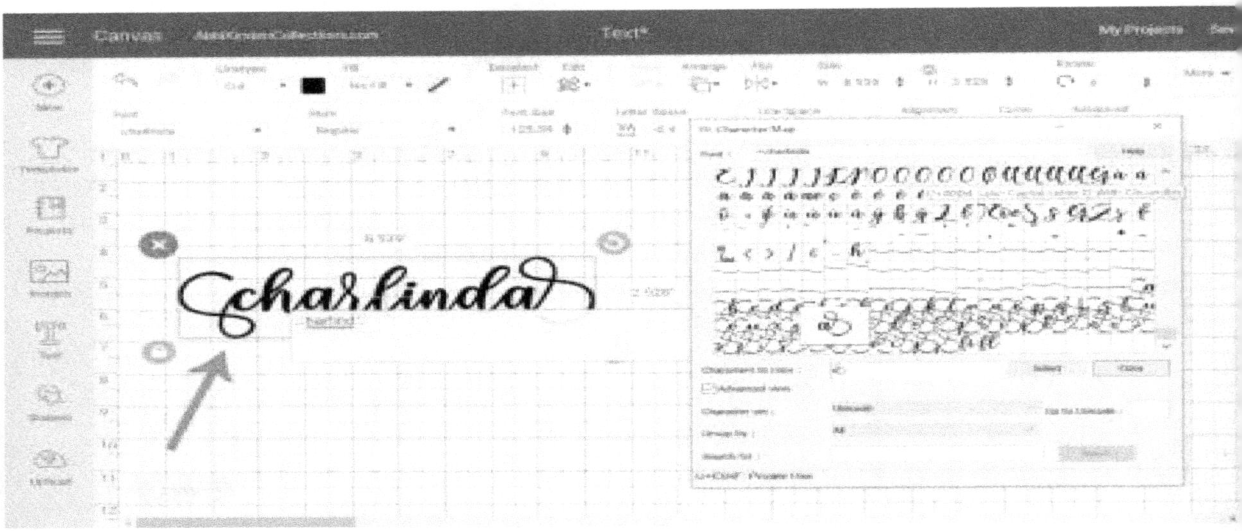

27. Maintain a list of your favorite vinyl records.

There is so much vinyl that it's difficult to keep track of them all! There are several styles, textures, and labels of vinyl to keep track of. To keep track, keep pieces of vinyl on a metal ring labeled with the brand and form of vinyl so you can still locate your favorite vinyl!

28. Keep supplies and machines in storage carts.

It's important to keep the supplies and machinery secure. A storage rolling cart is one of the favorite ways to do this! Check out your nearest Michaels shop!

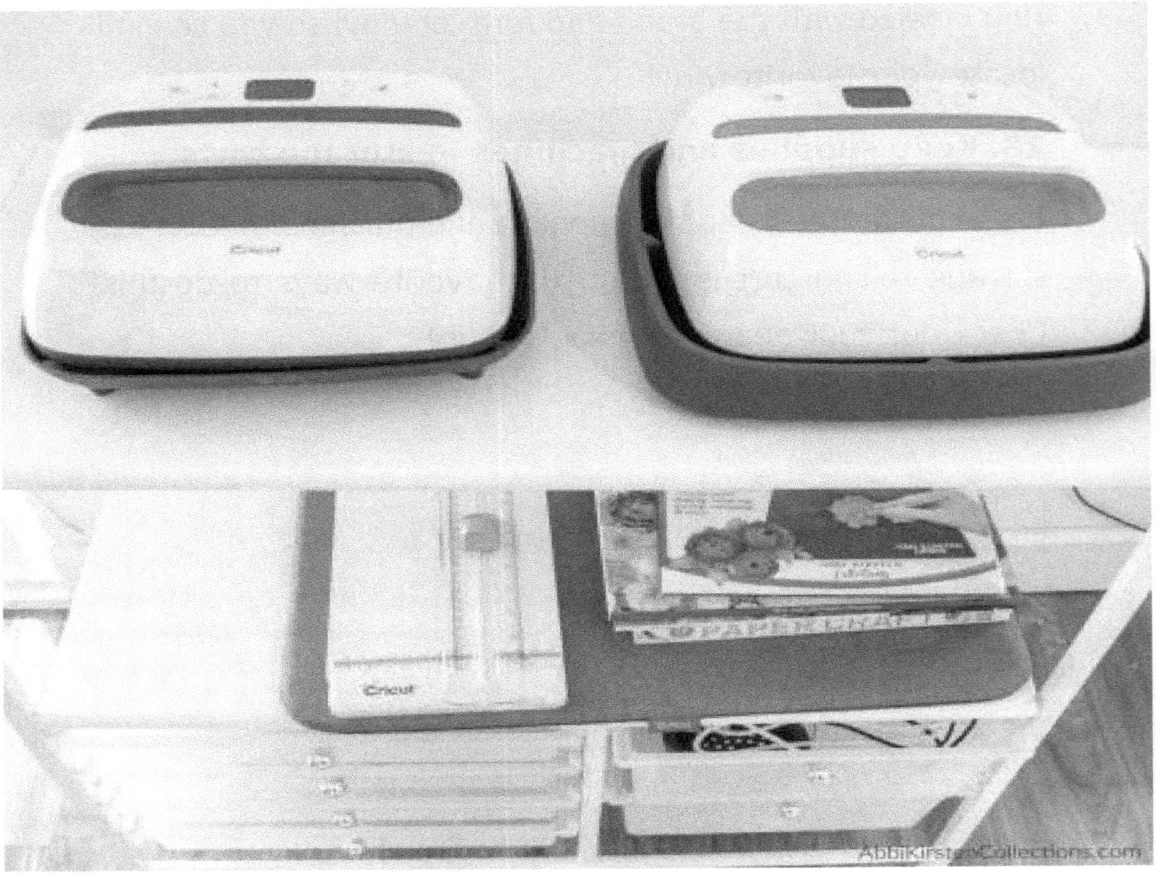

7.2 Mat Maintenance and Longevity

Since the mats are costly, you will want to retain them in service for a long time. The best way to extend the existence of a mat is to treat it carefully and properly. Here are some tips about how to take control of these mats:

• After each use, replace the transparent cover/film on the sheet. Which will keep the mat clean and free of dirt and dust.

• Use a lint roller to remove any substance debris from the mat surface during each use.

• Use non-alcoholic wipes to clean the mat.

• Wash the mats with soapy water, except for the silk mat. The cotton mat is unlike any other mat in that it cannot be washed with water.

• Using a scraper, clean any object debris from the mat surface except the cloth mat.

7.3 Cricut Maker Specialty Equipment

Aside from the blades, there are other specialized instruments for purposes other than cutting.

Markers and pens

There is a space for markers and pens next to the blade housing. If you want to design greeting cards and want to use elegant fonts, this is the place to go. The Cricut is compatible with a wide range of pens and markers. Markers and pens must be purchased separately.

Scoring Wheel

This is a one-of-a-kind feature. This scoring wheel is your buddy if you don't need to cut a pattern but only need to fold a piece of material. This feature can be used for a variety of things, like creating personalized crates and making a Greeting card.

Single and double scoring tips are the two forms of scoring tips available. Depending on the project, you will use the same housing with all styles of tips.

Fast Swap Housing and Helpful Tips

This is sole housing that can be used for a variety of feature tips. The tips that can be used colloquially with this housing are explained in the following section.

Foil Transfer Tip

This is one of the most recent Cricut Maker functions. This is used to embellish and bling up the finished products. It's designed to be used with foil covers.

Deboss tip

This tip is similar to the engraving tip, but it is designed for finer, lighter materials. Foil, dense card paper, and basswood may all be decorated with it.

Engrave tip

This tip may be used to engrave texts or monograms on a variety of items. Plastic mats, leather and metal sheets are the best materials for this. With this tip, you will make the projects more special.

Perforation Tip

Tear-off materials are often used for a project. The perforation tip is used for this reason. This tip works well for lightweight fabrics.

Wavy tip

This tip can come in handy when creating greeting cards. This results in wavy edges, which provide a decorative touch. It may be used to embellish card corners, as well as iron-on vinyl and other textured sheets.

Conclusion

Thank you for making it to the end. While you're reading this, it's reasonable to conclude with the various project information included in this book; you are ready to create new project ideas.

Crafting is fun, love, hobby and the best use of leisure time. But sometimes, it becomes hard and frustrating. For this, Cricut brings remarkable technology accompanied by so many machines, design software, materials, tools and accessories to make your design come true.

This guidebook was created to help you understand the potential of your Cricut device in terms of the designs it can create. Using a Cricut should be incredibly easy for you at this stage, and one of the main reasons that people prefer Cricut to do their cutting is that they are easy to use. If you have the proper tools, it's simple to use and understand. Since it is not overly complex, almost everyone can set a Cricut unit. What a potential customer has to do is obey the simple guidelines that arrive with the package.

So, you've mastered Cricut Design Space; you're a master crafter, what now? Why don't you bring your skills to good use? Now that you've seen a few examples of projects which can be done with a Cricut, you may have a few more ideas about how to utilize your latest gadget.

But bear in mind that you can never quit researching, attempting new ideas, or becoming imaginative. The Cricut does not make you any less innovative; it just simplifies the method such that you can devote your precious time and energy to more critical tasks, such as personalizing the ideas after they've been cut. It takes the boring work off your hands and turns it into something enjoyable, easy, and fast. Make your life, your house, and the homes of your companions more entertaining and built by using this!

Last but not least, keep in mind! You don't have to be a professional or an expert at making stuff. Give the Cricut a try to do the hard work for you, and you'll be pleased with the results.

I hope you've gained a lot of knowledge.

CPSIA information can be obtained
at www.ICGtesting.com
Printed in the USA
LVHW060917141021
700415LV00009B/45

9 781803 063904